How's Your Family?

How's Your Family?

A Guide to Identifying Your Family's Strengths and Weaknesses

by

JERRY M. LEWIS, M.D.

Director of Research,
Timberlawn Psychiatric Research Foundation,
Clinical Professor of Psychiatry,
University of Texas
Southwestern Medical School at Dallas

BRUNNER/MAZEL, *Publishers* • New York

Library of Congress Cataloging in Publication Data

Lewis, Jerry M., 1924–
  How's your family?
  1. Family. 2. Interpersonal relations. 3. Problem family. I. Title.

HQ734.L498   301.42   78-11820

ISBN 0-87630-181-2

Published by
BRUNNER/MAZEL, INC.
19 Union Square, New York, N.Y. 10003

MANUFACTURED IN THE UNITED STATES OF AMERICA

FOR

PAT

with love and gratitude

Contents

Acknowledgments

The material in this book has three sources. The first is the research study of families accomplished at the Timberlawn Psychiatric Research Foundation. My colleagues, W. Robert Beavers, M.D., John T. Gossett, Ph.D., and Virginia Austin Phillips, and I were equal partners in that endeavor, and we jointly presented the findings in a scientific publication.* The study was truly collaborative, but whatever credit is involved for that work we could not claim without the openness and generosity of the families who volunteered for the study.

The second source of material is clinical work with individuals, couples, and families who have come for help with problems growing out of their relationships with each other. What they taught me about the struggle to be a family has been indispensable in my coming to see the ways in which some families succeed and others fail.

The third source of material is a small group of friends and their families whose closeness has allowed us to share both the joys and the pains of family life.

And further, the writing itself requires an interpersonal network that supports, confronts, encourages, and criticizes. This writer's network included Virginia Austin Phillips and John T. Gossett, who offered encouragement, critique, and many valuable suggestions. W. Robert Beavers supported the concept that research findings should be passed on to the general reading audience. B. L. Mazel

---

* Lewis, J. M., Beavers, W. R., Gossett, J. T., and Phillips, V. A. *No Single Thread: Psychological Health in Family Systems.* Brunner/Mazel, Inc., New York, 1976. Further references in this book to our research refer to this volume.

supplied enthusiasm, urging me to transform an idea into a reality. Nannette Bruchey typed each draft and tracked down each reference with constant good humor.

Of course, the most vital support came from my own family. Pat, Jerry, Cynthia, Nancy, and Tom know that a part of each of them is here.

Introduction:

How's Your Family?

In a different and more perfect world, the family would be recognized as the unit of survival. People would think much more about their families and would treat them as their most valuable possession. Currently, many think about their families only when something goes wrong, and there is a likelihood then that the family members will focus on a symptom of family distress rather than on the cause of the distress. The idea of taking stock of one's family on a regular basis is rarely considered. The family automobile may be taken for a 20,000-mile checkup, family members may obtain yearly physical examination, corporations publish annual reports—but rarely is the family examined for its strengths and weaknesses.

In this volume we will look at how families function, focusing particularly on healthy families—families which promote the continued growth of the parents and produce healthy children. Characteristics that make for healthy functioning, as well as those which lead to trouble among family members, will be identified.

The material presented in this book lends itself to the examination of one's own family. Many readers may recognize their families in the descriptions of healthy, faltering, troubled, or severely troubled families. They may see their family as being strong in one area, such as solving problems, but weak in another, such as communicating on an intimate level.

It is hoped that this volume will help families to identify their strengths and weaknesses. As a first step in the process of evaluating one's family, it is suggested that the entire family or the marital couple answer the two brief questionnaires which follow. One applies to the whole family, and the other only to the parents' relationship. What is suggested is that each person answer each question privately and then the areas of agreement and disagreement can be discussed. This can provide a useful format both for the parents to discuss their relationship privately and for the whole family to participate in the appraisal of the family.

It is convenient to take a blank sheet of paper and place each question's number along the left margin. At the top should be written the four responses, "Does not apply at all," "Applies a little," "Applies a lot," and "Impossible to answer, don't know." The sheet of paper is now ready for use as the individual's score sheet. As with any questionnaire, greater understanding can be obtained if one does not hedge too much by using the "Applies a Little" response in questions where a more definite, "Applies a Lot" or "Does not Apply at All" would be more appropriate. It is often useful to use one's first thoughts as the answer, rather than spending a great deal of time thinking about each question. Finally, it is best to do the family appraisal at a "normal" or usual time in the life of the ftmily, rather than during a period of unusual stress.

Near the end of the volume, after we have looked at the characteristics of the healthy as well as troubled families, there will be an opportunity to compare your family's answers with the answers of healthy families. If you find that your family is already functioning at an optimal level, you can be justifiably proud. If your family evaluation leaves you feeling uneasy or troubled, let that feeling be the first step toward healthier family functioning.

WHOLE FAMILY QUESTIONNAIRE

IN OUR FAMILY:	Does not apply at all	Applies a little	Applies a lot	Impossible to answer, don't know

1. Both parents are the leaders. Neither is always dominant.
2. We can trust other family members not to hurt our feelings deliberately.
3. We believe that outsiders will often take advantage of us.
4. Relatives and friends usually take over when we're having trouble.
5. The children are encouraged to try new things.

6. We fight a lot.
7. Someone often acts as if he or she knows what I am thinking or feeling.
8. We often avoid facing problems until the last minute.
9. It is OK to express sadness.
10. Stress often leads to everyone going separate ways.

11. We are good at solving problems.
12. We don't have to feel ashamed of feelings.
13. We almost always talk about superficial things.
14. I can really be an individual.
15. We are supposed to let people know what our ideas are.

16. It is OK to express joy or happiness.
17. Our feelings don't get ridiculed or put down.
18. It is OK to have our own thoughts and ideas.
19. We are often angry.
20. We are encouraged to start new things.

21. Stress often results in one family member making all the decisions.
22. People let me know they've heard what I think and feel.
23. We are often sad or depressed.
24. It is OK to be interested in things that don't interest anyone else.
25. We often feel "what's the use?"

PARENTAL RELATIONSHIP QUESTIONNAIRE

IN OUR FAMILY:	Does not apply at all	Applies a little	Applies a lot	Impossible to answer, don't know
1. My wife (husband) and I can talk about our deep feelings and very private thoughts.				
2. I feel hopeless about ever getting what I need and want emotionally from my wife (husband).				
3. I find my wife (husband) physically attractive.				
4. My relationship with one of my parents or a friend is very special and, in some ways, closer than my relationship with my wife (husband)				
5. Sex with my wife (husband) is sometimes a very intimate, "together" experience.				
6. My personality and that of my wife (husband) seem to fit well together.				
7. My wife (husband) and I blame each other a lot.				
8. There is often tension in my relationship with my wife (husband).				
9. My relationship with one of our children is very special and, in some ways, closer than my relationship with my wife (husband).				
10. Sex with my wife (husband) is never really satisfactory.				
11. There is a strong "charge" or good feeling of excitement in my wife's (husband's) and my relationship.				
12. My wife (husband) and I are best friends.				
13. The most important part of my relationship with my wife (husband) is our children.				
14. I am often angry with my wife husband).				
15. Usually, my wife (husband) and I are openly affectionate with each other.				
16. Sex with my wife (husband) is sometimes a very fun experience.				
17. I know my wife (husband) cares deeply for me.				
18. Sex with my wife (husband) is sometimes a very tender experience.				
19. My wife (husband) and I have sex about as often as I want to.				
20. My relationship with my wife (husband) is the closest I've ever had.				

How's Your Family?

I

What the Healthy

Family Does

Imagine a world without families. Imagine that families had never been invented. Would there be a world? What would it be like? It is difficult to imagine such a world. Families seem a part of the whole business of being human. Anthropologists point out that even the very old forms of living together—hunting and gathering societies—had families. They speculate that families came into being about the time the human species evolved. The reason may be that families increased the likelihood of survival. There was a greater possibility that children would grow up, have children of their own, and keep the whole human species moving and growing.

The survival function of the family is so obvious that it may be overlooked. It still appears to be part of the job of the family. Even today, for example, people who live in families do better, on the average, than people who live alone. They live longer and have fewer illnesses. Although some may say that the reason for that is that healthier people have a greater tendency to marry and have families, that can't be the only explanation. People who lose their families don't do as well, on the average, as people who continue to live in families.

One report of the widespread loss of the family is the story of

HOW'S YOUR FAMILY?

lk.* These mountain people were torn out of their natural en-
ronment against their will and transported to a distant area. They
could no longer hunt and were introduced to farming. Having lost
control of their destiny, their society disintegrated. Families fell apart
and each individual was on his or her own. Relationships disappeared
and a mad scramble for individual survival ensued. Children and the
aged were left to die, and much of what has been considered human
nature evaporated. In all probability, the loss of family was both
cause and effect. However one interprets what happened, it is a
frightening picture of a world without families.

People need families, and need them for many reasons. Physical
survival, emotional support, protection, intimacy—the list could go
on and on. And, yet, families are so different in their capacities to
provide those essentials. Some families seem to do well, to be a
close-knit group with obvious affection for each other—and good
things frequently happen to them. Other families seem always to have
problems and troubles. One thing after another happens—and much
of it bad. Look around your neighborhood or consider the families
you know well. It is not usually difficult to identify both families
who do well and those who are troubled.

What are the differences? What accounts for the ability of some
families to do so well, while other families struggle and often fail to
provide their members with what they need? Some of the answers
to these questions have been clarified by recent research that focuses
on healthy as well as troubled families.

It is important, however, that the word "healthy" be clearly
defined. As used here, a healthy family is one that does two things
well: *preserves the sanity and encourages the growth of the parents*
and *produces healthy children*. Once you get beyond the family's
role in physical survival, that is what the family is all about.

A healthy family encourages the continued growth of each parent
—or, at the minimum, stabilizes each parent's personality. This fact
is too often unappreciated. Each person comes to marriage and the
creation of a family with certain problems—or, perhaps more accurately for most, certain vulnerabilities. Vulnerabilities are acquired

---

* Turnbull, Colin M. *The Mountain People.* Simon and Schuster, New York, 1972.

early in life. Some of them may be inherited tendencies or unusual temperaments. Many are acquired during the child's early development. Psychoanalysis and the broad field of childhood development have demonstrated that the early years of growth and development are complex and the emotional—as well as the physical—needs of the child—often are not completely met, frequently due to circumstances out of anyone's control. Since the child's developing sense of self is often fragile during these early years, many persons come to adulthood with a scar or two, a "soft spot," or aspects of the personality that are not as strong as they might be. Some individuals, more fortunate than most, have few. Many persons have a goodly number. Sometimes, the person is aware of his or her soft spots, but often the vulnerabilities are not conscious. If a particular life stress happens to hit upon a specific soft spot, the individual may develop anxiety, depression, or other forms of psychiatric disability.

Vulnerabilities, however, are—in and of themselves—not disabilities. People can live good and full lives with a number of soft spots. It is the conversion of vulnerabilities to disabilities that concerns us. It is in the stressful life circumstances we both face and create that vulnerabilities get converted to disabilities. For some, the stress is global, diffuse, ever-present—as in poverty, racial prejudice, or other forms of social deprivation. For others, however, the stresses are inside the family and grow out of daily conflict, smoldering resentments, crushed hopes, and, in general, the failure of the family to provide the support, acceptance, and meaning that each individual needs. It is, then, within the family that the individual's mental health is finally determined. At the least, vulnerabilities are not converted to disabilities, but much more is possible. In some families, the individuals' vulnerabilities are undone, past hurts are healed, and the quest to fulfill one's potential is encouraged.

The individual cannot change the past but, as an adult, has something to say about the kind of family he or she is going to have. This understanding, in contrast to the notion that *all* of what happens to one is laid down by heredity or early life circumstances, leads to a position of some optimism. As adults, we do have something to say about the future. By looking at and understanding our families and how they compare and contrast to healthy families, we can gain insight into the ways in which our families can offer us a better and less vulnerable future.

The connection between vulnerabilities from the past and disabilities can be illustrated with several examples from clinical practice.*

> Mary, a 31-year-old wife and mother, was seen by a psychiatrist because of a disabling depression. She felt worthless, hopeless, and had been unable to care for her two small children or manage her home for several months. Her early history revealed life circumstances often associated with great psychologic vulnerability. She was the older of two children of an alcoholic father and a mother who spent most of her time in a strict religious organization that emphasized conformity to a rigid code of rules. The family was often without adequate resources because of the father's job instability. Mary's mother, who was seen as a saint in the small town in which they lived, was rarely at home, and the care of the house and Mary's small brother fell to Mary at an early age.
>
> Psychologically, Mary needed a relationship in which she felt nourished and well cared for. She married Tom, a senior at the college located in the small town where she lived. Tom needed to take care of people and derived great satisfaction out of doing for others.
>
> During the ten years of their marriage, Tom and Mary had evolved a stable relationship. It was, however, one that seemed based on Tom's taking care of Mary.
>
> Mary's depression began shortly after Tom accepted a promotion that involved, for the first time, a great deal of travel. He was gone from home three or four nights most weeks. Tom and Mary had discussed his acceptance of the promotion and the travel that it involved, and Mary had encouraged him to take it because of what it promised for the future of their family.

In this clinical example, the nature of the couple's relationship provided the wife with considerable protection from her vulnerabilities from the past. However, the decreased emotional support the husband could provide directly because of his travel and increased job responsibilities was enough to tip the scale. What had

---

* Names and events in this and other examples have been altered in order to protect the confidentiality of the individuals involved.

been only a vulnerability was converted to a significant disability in the form of a serious depression.

Jim and Nancy and their family volunteered to participate in a research study of family life. Jim, a successful small businessman, was much more distant and remote than Nancy. He kept many feelings to himself and related this personality characteristic to the circumstances of his childhood. His parents had been killed in an accident when he was three, and he was raised by grandparents. He spent about equal time with each set of grandparents, but felt that neither set of grandparents really wanted the responsibility of raising him. Moving between grandparents involved frequent changes in schools and friends. Jim felt that he had become very cautious about revealing his feelings and getting close to people during those early years.

Nancy, on the other hand, came from a very tight-knit and close family. Jim and Nancy lived in the same section of a large city as her parents and brothers and sisters. She saw them daily, and was able to satisfy her need for emotional closeness and intimacy in those family relationships. As a consequence, she made few demands on Jim for emotional closeness. They had much in common, however, and their life together revolved around their children and shared interests in gardening, music, and a variety of other activities.

In this example, we can appreciate again the role that Jim and Nancy's relationship had in protecting Jim from his vulnerabilities. He feared emotional closeness and had "selected" a wife whose relationship with her own family provided her the opportunity for closeness. As a consequence, she made few demands on him for closeness, and in this way respected his need for a more distant type of relationship. If Jim had married a woman with greater needs for marital closeness or a less readily available family, there may well have been trouble. Whether either Jim or Nancy (or both) would have developed symptoms is a complicated question. For our purposes, however, the point is that Jim's vulnerability (fear of closeness) was not converted to a disability, as can be seen from the fact that neither Jim nor Nancy developed disabling symptoms.

Children may come into life with physical differences that can lead to vulnerabilities. Some families have the capacity to accept physical differences in children in a way that minimizes vulnerabilities.

The two older children in the Arnold family were much like the parents, both outgoing and athletic. John, the youngest child, was different. He was quiet and shy, and his physical movements appeared awkward. His birth had been difficult, and he had not been an easy infant to care for. However, his differences from the other members of the family were not seen as deficiencies. His interest in books and music was encouraged. His quiet and often wry comments were considered seriously and were obviously appreciated by other family members.

This family accepted their son's differences from the others in the family in ways that emphasized the positive aspects of his skills and talents. In another family, the child's physical differences from the family pattern might have been responded to in ways that would have resulted in severe disabilities for him.

It is this capacity of the family to be supportive that prevents vulnerabilities from becoming disabilities. It is important for both the parents and the children, but parents especially find in the family both the sense of meaning and the emotional closeness which are necessary to provide the chance for emotional growth as well as the protection from vulnerabilities out of the past.

The second job of the family involves encouraging the growth of the children in a way that allows each child to experience his or her individuality and to "leave" the family emotionally in order to love another. This is called "autonomy"—and it means the capacity to have one's own ideas, feelings, and life direction, to sense both one's differences from others and the ways in which one is like others, and to be able to initiate things. There are ways of being a family that encourage the growth of children toward separateness, individuality, and autonomy. Unfortunately, there are other ways of being a family that result in children who never develop any sense of separateness from their parents nor any clearly experienced individuality. The differences in such families can be seen in the following examples:

The Jacksons volunteered to participate in a research program studying family life. The parents and their children were warm, spontaneous, and very open with their feelings. The family, as a whole, encouraged each member to say clearly what he or she was thinking or feeling. In their family discussions, each person was clear and the observer had no difficulty knowing what the person was thinking or feeling. A typical dialogue would be:

Father: "What do all of you want to do on the 4th of July?"
Son: "Let's go to the ball game . . ."
Daughter: "A picnic on the beach . . ."
Mother: (laughing) "How about visiting your grandparents?"
Son: "We're only three games out of first place . . ."
Father: "Son, the gals don't enjoy baseball that much—it's our kind of thing, and on the 4th we all ought to do something together."
Daughter: "What about the beach?"
Mother: "I bet we'd all enjoy that—we can see your grandparents the next week."
Son: "OK."
Father: "Sounds like it's settled."

In this example, each person expressed himself or herself clearly. There is no problem knowing what each of them thinks and feels. It is the encouragement of this type of clear expression that helps children grow up with a real sense of their own individuality. This is one of the ways that a family encourages children to be individuals who ultimately can lead their own separate lives. Contrast this family conversation with that from a different family:

Father: "What do you want to do today?"
Son: "Well—what about the beach . . ."
Daughter: "It'll be hot."
Mother: "We could go late to avoid . . ."
Father: "I kind of thought . . ."
Son: "It might be crowded."
Father: "Maybe it will rain."
Mother: "There's a good movie at the Granada."
Daughter: "Susie is coming over."

In this family conversation, it is difficult to know what the individuals think and feel. The family does not insist on the clear expression of feelings and thoughts. Children growing up in an environment where so little clear expression is encouraged may have greater difficulty in sensing their individuality. As a result, there may be a greater tendency to avoid separating from the family and leading lives of their own.

Throughout this book, the term "healthy" refers to families that do the two important jobs of the family well. They stabilize or promote growth in the parent's personalities, and raise children who achieve high levels of individuality and autonomy. What is presented grows out of our research study of a group of such families. The families were studied in their homes, at the research center, and at their places of business. They were studied by interviewing the individuals, administering psychological tests to the individuals, interviewing the whole family, and by the use of special testing procedures that measured both the way in which the parents communicated with each other and the way in which the whole family communicated and solved problems.

These research volunteer families, as well as the troubled families also described in this book, represented only a particular group of families. It seems important to call the reader's attention to the limits of generalization safely possible. The restricted sample of families is both a weakness and a strength. Although generalizations to all sorts of families cannot be made, what can be said about the kinds of families studied can be stated with assurance. The lessons for the reader are dependent upon the degree to which the reader's family is like the families studied in regard to certain broad characteristics. The families described here, with few exceptions, were white, Protestant, and middle- or upper-middle-class socioeconomically. They were biologically intact families whose oldest child was in adolescence. As such, there is no way of knowing whether the findings apply to other families.

The families studied were protected from many life stresses by virtue of their economic success and position in the mainstream of American life. They did not have to deal with poverty, prejudice, or other forms of social deprivation. Recently, Keniston has emphasized the terrible impact on the family of broad social and economic forces over which the family has no control.* He stresses that the family is not truly self-sufficient and must depend upon the

---

* Keniston, Kenneth. *All Our Children.* Harcourt, Brace, Jovanovich, New York, 1977.

outside world for many important functions. His call is for broad social changes in order to alter the context in which too many families suffer. One can be in firm agreement with Keniston's call, and yet be interested in the factors that are associated with different levels of competence in families who appear to have the greatest opportunity for health in contemporary America.

It is hoped that the descriptions of healthy and troubled families will provide the reader with a framework in which to look at his or her family. This can be painful if it is apparent that one's family is much more like the description of troubled families than like the portrayal of healthy families. The pain, however, can become the impetus to change. Change in the family is possible if one knows in what ways the family is not functioning well and the direction required to move the family towards more effective or healthy functioning. Too often, individuals do not take the time, nor can they tolerate the pain involved in assessing their families. They take the family for granted, and it is easier to blame others ("my husband," "my wife," "my in-laws") than it is to honestly evaluate the family situation. There is a world of difference between blaming others and sitting down with them and saying, "*We* have some problems—can we look at them together?" Starting with "we" may allow the discussion to proceed beyond the initial and defeating phase of blaming each other.

It takes courage and time to change. Families develop patterns of relating and communicating over months and years, and the patterns usually cannot be suddenly discarded. It takes courage to try, for change often seems unpredictable and risky.

The Becketts were in their sixties when they came for help with their marriage. For 30 years, Gladys had been "the patient," and, because of anger, depression, abuse of alcohol, and other symptoms, she had been admitted on numerous occasions to psychiatric hospitals and had received many years of outpatient psychotherapy (she blamed her husband's lack of affection for her difficulties). Her husband, Sanford, was a successful man who had achieved great wealth. He was a quiet, intense, proper man who seemed unable to deal openly with feelings. He saw the problem as entirely his wife's illness. The marital relationship had deteriorated over the years, and for the four years before being seen together, they had been living separate lives, although sharing the same home. At this point, Sanford, for the first time, felt depressed and agreed to try marital therapy, and Gladys reluctantly acquiesced. The treatment did not focus on their long-standing problems, but was a directive, educational approach in which each agreed to begin meeting simple requests made by the other. This approach was beneficial, and over a few months both were feeling better and agreed that their relationship was "better than in many years," and that they were happy.

Although this couple's response to outside help was unusually quick and dramatic, that is not the focus of this clinical example. Rather, I would emphasize the courage it took both of these people to change the pattern of years of blaming each other, severe conflict, mutual anger, and prolonged hopelessness about ever getting what they wanted from each other. After the improvement in their relationship, each shared that this was to be the "last chance."

The descriptions of healthy and troubled families will bring pain to some readers. However, it is hoped that the pain, combined with courage and the realization that it is possible to change, will result in renewed hope for many.

II

It Starts with Marriage

In talking with young people who ask, "What can I do to be a psychologically healthy person?" I answer, "Most of all, marry well." Although many things go into the making of a healthy family, none is more important than the nature of the parents' marriage. It is difficult for a family to be healthy if the parents' relationship is severely troubled most of the time. In fact, there is evidence that the quality of the relationship may be more important than the individual personalities of the parents in determining the health of the family. One study, for example, revealed that psychologically healthy children could emerge from two different types of families.* In one, both parents were healthy individuals and they shared a warm, caring, and good relationship. In the second type of family, one parent had obvious emotional problems, but the relationship between the parents was warm and mutually supportive. If, however, the parents' relationship was a constantly conflicted one, there was less likelihood that the children would turn out to be healthy.

Another study noted the supportive aspect of a good marriage for men.* Those men who were seen as well-adjusted had made a stable marriage before 30 and were still very much involved with their wives 20 years later.

* Westley, W. A., and Epstein, N. B. *The Silent Majority*. Jossey-Bass, Inc., San Francisco, 1969.
* Vaillant, G. D. *Adaptation to Life*. Little, Brown, and Co., Boston 1977.

13

There is also evidence that a conflicted, nonsupportive marriage may be the immediate cause of a severe emotional breakdown for adults. One study, for example, revealed that persons with severely deprived childhoods developed severe mental illness only if their marriages failed to provide security and acceptance. Individuals with similar childhood deprivation did not develop mental illness if their marriages were supportive.* Another study explored the role of marital conflict in precipitating depression in women.** Having a marital relationship in which psychologic intimacy is possible offers protection against the development of depression even if stress from other sources is severe.***

It appears, therefore, that the nature of an individual's marital relationship may play an important role in determining the quality of the person's life. It may influence the individual's personal mental health directly and also have profound impact on the quality of life in the family.

If the quality of a marriage is so often crucial for both husband and wife and contributes critically to the overall health of the family, it is important to understand the kind of factors involved in the decision to marry. Individuals looking back at marriages which failed make the following kinds of statements.

"I thought I could help him find himself. He was lonely and seemed to lack direction."

"We fought constantly before we got married—it was one huge battle. I am not sure why I felt it would be different after we got married."

"I knew she was strong and dominant like my mother—but she seemed so certain it was going to work."

"I kind of knew he drank too much, but it didn't seem all that important then."

"It was one of those whirlwind things—we met at Thanksgiving and married at Christmas. We really didn't know each other at all."

---

* Rogler, Lloyd H., and Hollingshead, August B. *Trapped: Families and Schizophrenia.* John Wiley and Sons, Inc., New York, 1965.

** Weissmann, M. M., and Paykel, E. S. *The Depressed Woman: A Study of Social Relationships*, University of Chicago Press, Chicago, 1974.

*** Brown G., Bhrolchain, M., and Harris, T. Social class and psychiatric disturbance among women in an urban population. *Sociology*, 9:225-259, 1975.

"My period was late and I was too embarrassed to go to the doctor—so we just decided to get married instead."

"Well, it seemed that all my friends were getting married—I felt kind of lonely maybe—it just seemed time to get married."

"She was so different from anyone I had ever known—not at all like my family or friends—it was exciting to be with someone different."

These statements tell us something about how little individuals may know about the factors that influence the decision to marry. The question remains, "Why does a person decide to marry a particular other?" Many would answer the question simply, "Because two people fell in love with each other." That answer is less than helpful because no one understands what love is. Definitions of romantic love vary from "the most sublime state a person is capable of" to "temporary insanity." However, the factors that influence the decision to marry a particular person seem to fall into three different categories. A very powerful one involves *social or background factors*. More often than not, individuals who marry share similar backgrounds—educational, religious, cultural, and economic. One of the reasons appears to be that similarities in background factors often are associated with similar values. The fact that two people agree about what is important in life—what life is supposed to be under the best circumstances—tends to act as an attracting force. It brings them together; it puts them in touch with one another.

A second aspect of an individual's choice of mate involves *personal characteristics*. Different people are stimulated by different characteristics in others, but at any one period of time in a culture there are some preferred characteristics, and both men and women are subtly conditioned as to what is desirable in the opposite sex. At this time, for example, baldness in men and obesity in women are not valued highly, although they may have been in the past or may come to be in the future.

Don Jackson, a pioneer family researcher, once told me that if you want to measure the quality of a marriage and can ask only one question of each partner, ask, "Out of the millions of people in the world, why did you marry your spouse?" Then listen for any reference in the answer to something personal about the spouse. It doesn't matter whether it is a physical characteristic or personality feature; if it is particular to that person, there is a better likelihood of a good marriage than if there is no personal reference in the response. Intrigued by the tongue-in-cheek simplicity of Jackson's suggestion, I have included the question in research interviews with patients admitted to a general hospital. The first interview was with a middle-aged rancher who had been admitted because of the possibility of heart disease. After about 45 minutes of the interview, I asked him Jackson's question. He looked at me as if I was out of my mind and responded as if any fool would know, "She lived in the same county."

Jackson's question attempts to determine the specific features of the other that aroused or excited the individual. The answer can be understood as both a rough gauge of what it was that stirred the feelings of the individual and of the intensity of the feelings that were aroused. That rancher's answer really did reflect the sterile, unemotional nature of his unsatisfactory marriage.

Most people would agree with the commonsense notion that a similar background and shared values, along with desirable physical or personality features, are important in the decision about whom to marry. There is less understanding regarding the role played by factors of which the individuals are unaware. However, work with couples strongly supports the role of such unconscious factors in the decision about whom to marry.

The idea that an individual may be attracted to another person by unconscious forces operating in his or her personality grows out of the observations made by therapists and counselors in working with distressed individuals and couples. Repeatedly, therapists see couples who, as individuals, have opposite personality traits that appear to "fit" each other. One spouse may be shy, the other outgoing; one may be a dominant person, the other submissive; one may be aggressive, the other passive. This tendency is often called "complementarity." If the fit meets their individual needs, it produces a smooth and integrated relationship. However, as individuals change, the complementary differences may come to make life miserable. In either event, it is rare to find couples who are fully aware of their opposite, complementary traits. Although some complementary traits develop after marriage, most often such traits were present to some extent from the start and influenced the decision to marry.

> Howard and Judith Allen married shortly after he graduated from medical school. He was a quiet, bright, and passive man who found Judith's aggressive competence pleasing. She made most of their decisions and was comfortable being in control. Ten years later, Howard began to feel dissatisfied with his life. He was a member of a large medical group, and most of the decisions were made by senior partners. At home, Judith ran everything—the children, their investments, and decisions about the home, vacations, and all aspects of family life.
>
> Howard began to resent Judith, his senior partners, and everyone who seemed to dictate to him. He wanted to be "his own man," and gradually became involved with a young and very dependent woman. He left the medical group without clear plans for a professional future. It was at this point that he and Judith requested help with their problems.

This couple was attracted to each other by strong differences which initially appeared complementary. He needed a strong woman, and she was happy with a man who needed her aggressiveness. However, their "fit" was altered by his discontent. His gradual maturation resulted in the need to feel that he was capable of greater independence. Although the directions he took were of questionable effectiveness, their marital therapy soon focused on whether Judith could begin to share power with Howard. What had once been complementary was no longer so and, if the relationship was to survive, some of its basic features would need to change.

The attraction of complementary differences can be a strong pull toward some relationships. In such instances, it may be referred to as a need—"he needs a submissive woman" or "she needs a dominant man." Hemingway described such a relationship in his short story, "The Short and Happy Life of Francis Macomber."* In this story, the wife "needed" a cowardly man and, although not openly admiring that trait, she could not tolerate the development of his courage.

---

* Hemingway, Ernest. "The Short and Happy Life of Francis Macomber," in *The Snows of Kilimanjaro and Other Stories*. Charles Scribner and Sons, New York, 1969.

In addition to (and sometimes related to) the attraction of persons whose personality characteristics appear to fit in a complementary way, early experiences with parents during childhood may influence the selection of mates. Often, individuals are not aware of such influences. There are several patterns. The healthiest is that in which a child is exposed to a good parental marriage. In such a marriage, each parent respects the other; both are important. The relationship is gratifying to both, and neither needs a charged, emotional coalition outside the marriage. This type of marriage serves as a model for the developing child. He or she comes to feel that such a relationship is natural, and later feels a strong (but often unconscious) lure to establish a marital relationship with similar characteristics. In this way, there is a strong tendency for good marriages to be transmitted from generation to generation.

Currently, 15 percent of children in this country are being raised by a single parent. In the great majority, the mother is the only parent. Mavis Hetherington has studied one facet of the impact of this circumstance in her study of the daughters of divorced and widowed women.* She found that the daughters of divorced mothers more frequently had negative thoughts of men in general, and often they married men who confirmed the negative image—that is, men who were unstable, did not hold jobs well and, in general, were poor husbands. The daughters of widowed mothers had less negative images of men in general, and tended to marry older, stable men who were good husbands. Although there are, of course, many exceptions to this finding, the tendency was impressive. It is important to emphasize that the young women involved did not consciously and deliberately select different types of husbands, although their feelings about the manner in which they lost their fathers appeared to influence their selection of mates.

Norman Paul, a psychiatrist, has suggested that marriage can be understood as an attempt by the individual to heal himself or herself.** He refers to the need many persons have to work out with a

---

* Hetherington, E. Mavis. Effects of father absence on personality development in adolescent daughters. *Developmental Psychology*, 7(3):313-326, 1972.

** Paul, Norman L. and Paul, Betty Byfield. *A Marital Puzzle*. W. W. Norton, New York, 1975.

spouse feelings and problems that have been left over from their childhood relationships with parents. Several examples will illustrate this process.

Alice, the only daughter of a successful surgeon, had four older brothers. She had a very special relationship with her father; in his eyes she could do no wrong. Within the family, she was like a little princess whose every wish was fulfilled. She married a medical student who was the older and only brother to three sisters. In his own family, he looked after his sisters and treated them with great consideration. Thus, Alice "selected" a husband who continued the pattern of her specialness, and her young husband "selected" a woman who needed the only kind of relationship he was accustomed to having with women.

In this example, neither Alice nor her husband had any inner reason to avoid perpetuating earlier patterns in their relationship with each other. That is because the earlier relationship patterns were comfortable and not significantly conflicted. Often, however, there is considerable inner turmoil about the relationship which may influence the selection of a mate.

Jack came from a family in which his mother was the powerful and dominant person. She overwhelmed Jack's father and made all the decisions for her children. Jack joined the Air Force immediately after completing high school. Several years later, he met Joan, and they married. Joan was an attractive but very passive and dependent woman who needed to feel cared for by a strong person. Jack and Joan's relationship was stormy from the start, and most of their conflicts appeared to center about Joan's insistence that Jack make all decisions and take the entire responsibility for their life together.

In this example, Jack has brought to the relationship his conflicted relationship with his mother. He wished to avoid a relationship with a domineering woman, yet he was insecure about handling most of the responsibility within the relationship. His "choice," Joan, allowed him to avoid the powerful mother-wife he feared, but he was anxious and insecure with all the power and responsibility. Consequently, they were always dissatisfied with each other; he was critical of both her dependency and her rare attempts to be more independent, and she was repelled both by his demands that she be more independent and by his failure to be a strong father figure to her.

The impact of an earlier relationship with a parent on the selection of a spouse does not necessarily involve the parent of the same sex as the spouse. A man's relationship with his father or a woman's with her mother may influence the selection of a mate.

> Mary was the only child of a remote, cold, and nearly reclusive mother. She never felt certain about her mother's love, and as she grew older came to resent the great distance she felt in her relationship with her mother. She was strongly attracted to Fred in high school. He was warm and very expressive. They married soon after graduating, and their relationship has been a satisfying one.

In this example, Mary "selected" a husband whose warmth and expressiveness provided her with the type of relationship she had missed with her mother.

As we have seen, there is evidence that in selecting each other as mates, many individuals are influenced by earlier relationships with parents. Under the best circumstances, a person may "select" a spouse with whom the healthy interactions learned from parents can be repeated. Others, however, search for a spouse with whom either a special relationship with a parent can be relived or a painful relationship can be healed. In many marriages, there is some degree of complementarity or "fit" of both partners' needs. In the absence of a good "fit," there is a strong likelihood of marital conflict.

These often unconscious factors, along with shared background and values and personal characteristics attractive to each other, appear to play a decisive role in how two people come together and decide to marry.

There are critical issues to be faced during courtship and early marriage. One involves the completion of the process of emotional separation from each spouse's parents and family of origin. The second issue is the necessity for the couple to work out the rules of their evolving relationship.

BEING BOSS OR GETTING CLOSE

Each couple must work out two aspects of their relationship—power and intimacy. Although these issues are rarely discussed openly and with deliberateness, they must be dealt with. Usually, a pattern established during courtship continues to evolve during the early years of marriage. At any rate, it is impossible *not* to deal with these dimensions of a relationship.

Power, in the sense used here, refers to the capacity of each partner to influence the other—to make his or her thoughts and feelings the prevailing force in the countless decisions the couple faces. In this sense, power is concerned with the answer to the question, "Who has the right to make what decisions?" Most couples evolve guidelines or rules which govern decision-making, although these rules are not often formally discussed.

> "Come to think about it, we never actually discussed the fact that we had to agree about big purchases—like a refrigerator or car—it just worked out that way. Jim seems happy enough if I buy a lamp without discussing it with him, and he buys power tools without asking me about it. I guess if it costs more than about $100 we have agreed somehow to talk about it beforehand."

> "Mary likes the mountains and I prefer the beach. On vacations we alternate—just started doing it that way—but we never really talked about it—it just kind of happened."

> "We just worked it out somehow. Jane has always been into the stock market—it fascinates her, and she's very knowledgeable. Gradually, she just took over most of the responsibility for what few investments we can make. She always discusses the stocks with me, but we both know she's the expert, and her opinion counts more than mine."

These individuals were talking about the rules that evolved in their marriages. The rules concerned the way in which certain decisions were made. In this sense, the individuals were talking about the way power was distributed within their relationship. There are a variety of patterns possible: a more-or-less equal sharing of power, a dominant-submissive distribution, a warfare state, and a fused condition.

In the *more-or-less equal* distribution of power, both individuals are competent, and each has areas of expertise in which his or her views may have greater weight. In this way, the circumstances influence which partner takes the leadership role. Often, the areas of expertise fall into traditional categories—home and children for women and the outside world for men. However, it is not unusual for the areas of expertise to fall outside of traditional, sex-linked roles. The husband who does most of the cooking and the wife who is more knowledgeable about investments are two examples. Regardless of the distribution of power, the important feature of this pattern is that each individual sees the other (and perceives himself or herself) as competent.

The *dominant-submissive* pattern of marital power distribution is found when one partner's views prevail regardless of the circumstances. All the expertise is assumed to be within the individual, and his or her thoughts and feelings dictate the decision-making in every situation. This is the classical "one-up one-down" type of relationship. Some couples find this pattern acceptable. Under such circumstances, there is little, if any, open conflict, and the relationship is a highly complementary one—that is, both persons' needs are met by the relationship. But often there is some degree of underlying conflict that, from time to time, erupts into the open. Frequently, this is related to the anger the submissive partner experiences. Never feeling competent and always giving in to the other lead to diminishing self-esteem and anger directed at the dominant mate. Occasionally, the conflict may start with the dominant partner's weariness with the unending responsibility of always being in charge of everything. He or she then becomes angry at the spouse for the dilemma. When couples with a conflicted, dominant-submissive relationship enter marital therapy, often each participant can see only the other's contribution to the problem. A dominant husband, for example, can resent his wife's submissive dependency without any appreciation of how much he has invited or pushed her into that role. In the same way, a submissive wife can offer countless real examples of her husband's heavy-handed dominance, with no awareness of the way her passive, dependent, or submissive behavior has encouraged the very behavior that hurts and angers her.

The *warfare* state marriage is one of constant and open conflict. Couples with this pattern of power have been unable to achieve any sort of stable equilibrium. Each individual seeks a dominant position, and neither person accepts a submissive role. They are intensely competitive, with a mutual theme of "I can do anything better than you can." The balance of power shifts from moment to moment, and each spouse appears willing to do anything to put the other down and gain the upper hand—however short-lived the apparent victory.

In a *fused* relationship, the partners share power, but the sharing is at the cost of relinquishing individual identity. Separateness—in the sense of personal thoughts or feelings—is dangerous, and a sticky "we-ness" permeates the relationship. "We always feel and think alike," one husband said, without realizing the loss of individual identity involved.

These four patterns of power distribution within marital relationships can be seen as points on a curve or graph of marital competence. They overlap, and "pure" types are not always apparent. The patterns are important for several reasons. Despite the possibility that the individuals involved can be relatively satisfied with any of the four patterns, there is an overall greater possibility of mutual satisfaction with the pattern of equal or nearly equal power. The reason for this is that psychological intimacy is a greater possibility when both spouses are seen as competent or powerful.

Within a marital relationship, communication occurs at a number of levels. Most commonly, couples talk at the level of events. They report things that happened to them, or occurrences each observed. Another level involves ideas. Many couples exchange thoughts, plans, and hopes in the form of ideas. Some couples talk freely about their everyday feelings and daydreams. The level of intimate communication occurs when each individual is able to share deep feelings and very personal thoughts and is able to listen and be "with" the other at this level. The capacity of the couple to achieve this level of sharing—at least on some occasions—is the core of intimacy. It is a reciprocal process—the mutual exchange of private worlds. Basically, it involves a willingness to expose vulnerabilities—to take the chance that sharing deep feelings and thoughts will not lead to rejection or be misused.

People enter adult life with very different capacities for intimacy. Some people cannot risk this type of closeness, and all relationships must involve considerable distance. Such people are always on guard and must always be in control. To them, to be vulnerable, to share one's private world, seems too dangerous.

If marital partners see each other as competent, deeper levels of intimacy can develop. There is little risk. If the relationship is a dominant-submissive one, both the dominant and submissive individuals have reasons to avoid intimacy. The dominant spouse fears that sharing doubts, fears, or uncertainties will be interpreted as weakness and used against him or her. The submissive spouse, already feeling inadequate, is afraid of being put down further by the disclosure of private thoughts and feelings.

Warfare marriage is a relationship in which intimacy is impossible. Each spouse correctly identifies the other's readiness to use any information in the chronic battle. To share one's private world is to invite attack.

The fused relationship involves a particular kind of sharing. Here, the thrust is for sameness—any difference threatens. So long as each spouse thinks and feels what he or she suspects the other thinks or feels, there can be considerable sharing. On the occasions, however, when the individuals do not feel and think as one, either or both may go to extraordinary extremes to avoid experiencing the differences. At times, this may even involve the denial of reality—a kind of shared craziness.

Because the way in which a couple deals with power in their relationship affects their level of intimacy, this area is most crucial in determining the quality of the marriage. But not everyone wishes either to feel competent or to be intimate with another. For such individuals, the needs of the persons they marry are critical to the success of the match. If they "select" a person whose needs for intimacy are greater or less than their own, one of them must deal with painful loneliness. If they participate in the development of a relationship in which power is not shared, they have diminished greatly the possibility of deep levels of intimacy.

Power and intimacy can be seen, then, as two critical issues that must be dealt with in every marriage. By now, one thing is clear—

one cannot be the boss in the sense of having tremendous power and, at the same time, be close to the other person. The two just don't go together that way.

The differences that these patterns of power distribution can make in dealing with a common problem can be demonstrated by typical conversations couples have. Let us assume that a couple's only child, a 14-year-old daughter, has been invited to a school dance by a 17-year-old boy. She has shared her excitement about the invitation with her mother, who wishes to discuss the matter with her husband.

A Couple With Shared Power:

> *Mother*: "Jim, we have a problem."
> *Father*: "Eh?—What's up?"
> *Mother*: "Sally has been asked to the prom."
> *Father*: "Oh ... gee ... she's just a kid."
> *Mother*: "Honey, she's 14—and some of her friends have been asked."
> *Father*: "It seems awfully young to me ..."
> *Mother*: "I know—it's scary."
> *Father*: " It really makes me nervous to think about it."
> *Mother*: "She's so excited—I remember how it was when I was asked out for the first time."
> *Father*: "Who's the boy?"
> *Mother*: "That Brinen boy down the street—a nice kid—but he does drive ..."
> *Father*: "That really shakes me up—I don't know how to respond. Part of me is happy for Sally—but a big part of me is scared and wants to say, 'No—not until you're older ...' "
> *Mother*: "I'm with you—I have both kinds of feelings. What shall we do—sleep on it?"
> *Father*: "Yes—I'd rather not decide right now—let's both think about it and then we can decide tomorrow."
> *Mother*: "OK—what's on television?"

A Couple With a Dominant-Submissive Relation:

> *Mother*: "Jim, we have a problem."
> *Father*: "Eh?—What's up?"
> *Mother*: "Sally has been asked to the prom ..."
> *Father*: "That's no problem."
> *Mother*: "She's very excited—some of her friends have been asked."

Father: "You're not serious? She's only 14!"
Mother: "I think we ought to consider it."
Father: "Mary, you're out of your mind—she's 14 and can't go."
Mother: "Jim—let's not decide quickly ..."
Father: "Damn—you don't understand what's going on in the world. You don't know what boys are after—there isn't any use in discussing it. I've made up my mind—she's not going—period. It's settled. Now, let's see what's on television."

A Warfare State Couple

Mother: "Jim—Sally has been invited to the prom and I think she ought to go. Some of her friends are going ..."
Father: "Are you crazy? She's only 14—you must be out of it."
Mother: "Don't call me crazy ..."
Father: "Damn it—if you'd only be reasonable once in a while."
Mother: "Me? Hell—you've got your mind made up before you hear about something—your mind is always closed. You never think anything through ..."
Father: "Me? You never change your mind. Your father told me you've been stubborn all your life—there isn't really any use discussing it."
Mother: "That's your style—just walk away from any problem. Never make a decision if you can avoid it ..."
Father: "Why don't you shut up ..."

The Fused Couple

Mother: "Jim, Sally has been invited to the prom and wants to know what we think."
Father: "Well—what do you think?"
Mother: "I've wondered about it ..."
Father: "It's difficult—she's only 14, but I suppose we might ..."
Mother: "We might ..."
Father: "Yeah ..."
Mother: "Are we settled on it?"
Father: "I guess. We seem together on it."
Mother: "I have that feeling."
Father: "What's on television?"
Mother: "What do we want to watch—the movie or the talk show?"

These examples are brief, but they demonstrate the quality of typical conversations of couples with different patterns of power distribution. The ones with shared power were able to tell each other more about their feelings, and their decision was a mutual one. The dominant-submissive couple reached a quick decision, but it reflected only the feelings and thoughts of the dominant husband, and his underlying fears were only indirectly mentioned. The warfare state couple really did not deal with the issue, but quickly became involved in another round of their endless conflict. The fused couple was concerned more with avoiding difference than with the issue of their daughter. Their conversation was typically vague and meaning unclear.

Power and intimacy are key issues that underlie every marriage. "Who has the right to decide what?" and "How close can we be?" are the questions that each couple must answer. More often than not, they do so without understanding clearly that they are establishing a pattern that will influence every day of their life together.

III

Putting It All Together —
the Good Marriage

What are the factors that go into the making of a good marriage? Shared power and intimacy are cornerstones and, for many couples, sexuality is a third important dimension. In this chapter, I will describe the marriages we studied that appear to work best. They are associated with high levels of mental health for both husband and wife, and bring great satisfaction to both. They are correlated also with a level of family life that produces healthy children.

SHARING POWER

The marriages that were working extremely well were relationships in which power was shared. Both wife and husband were competent and capable of providing the family with leadership. Often, the areas of competence complemented each other, and there was little, if any, competition in the relationship. The parental coalition was effective and the inevitable differences were dealt with quickly and with efficiency. These couples negotiated well. Each individual was able to state opinions clearly and to express a wide range of feelings. That they could differ agreeably was apparent early in the couple's discussions. Neither partner assumed automatically that he or she had a monopoly on the truth, the "right" way to feel, or the "inside" information. Rather, each respected the viewpoint of the other and listened carefully. If a consensus could not be reached, these couples were good at compromising. There was no suggestion of major differences in each individual's power or influence and, as a result, neither was either consistently dominant or submissive.

As a consequence of this easy sharing of power, there was no evidence that either spouse needed an alliance with another person. There was not the kind of strong parent-child coalition found in some distressed families. Neither was there a powerful coalition between either husband or wife and one of their parents nor, for that matter, with anyone outside the family. If both partners feel powerful and respected within the marital relationship, there is little need for a powerful ally outside the marriage.

INTIMACY

A second important aspect of these marriages is the "in love" quality of the relationship. Most of the couples studied had been married for 15-20 years, but there was still a strong charge to the relationship. They cared about each other, and the "juice" or "electricity" in the relationship was clearly apparent. Related to this was the presence of high levels of intimacy.

> "I've never been this close to anyone—I can let him know what I really feel."

> "It's wonderful to be able to discuss everything with her—no holding back—no fears of ridicule or rejection."

> "There are times when what I feel seems silly—some insecurity or something—but I let him know about it—and he is the same way. Usually, it's at night and we're talking in bed—I tell you, it's really great to go to sleep after that kind of sharing."

Intimacy, in the sense used here, involves the capacity of each person to be deeply empathic with the other; to be momentarily in the other's shoes; to let the other know that one understands what he or she is feeling. In this way, both husband and wife are able to feel deeply cared for and understood. There is little reason, therefore, to seek a "special" relationship—an emotionally charged coalition with someone else. First of all, we found no such "special" relationship between either husband and wife and any of their children. In troubled families, one often finds a charged father-daughter or mother-son relationship. In these alliances, there are higher levels of psychological intimacy than exist in the parental relationship.

Neither did we find "special" relationships with outsiders. Although the individuals had good and close relationships with friends and relatives, there was no evidence that these relationships were needed to substitute for an emotionally deficient marriage. Clinical work with couples with troubled relationships suggests, as a contrast, that an extramarital affair is prompted often by the feeling of being inadequately understood within the marriage.

It appears, therefore, that involvement in a marriage in which power is shared and intimacy available precludes the need for a special coalition either within or outside the family. One needs neither an ally nor a lover if one has both in a spouse.

The nature of these relationships was particularly impressive when considered in the light of how busy these men and women were. They were very involved with their children and considerable energy and time went into family activities. The activities themselves were diverse and ranged from athletic participation to cultural or artistic endeavors. The mothers, most of whom did not work outside the home, were involved in a variety of neighborhood and civic affairs. The fathers, all of whom were successful at work, invested much of themselves in their work. They described work satisfactions as primarily people-oriented, and many spent far more than 40 hours per week on the job. As a group, however, they had a good deal of themselves left over for their wives and families. This point deserves emphasis because it is one of the clear differences between these families and families seen as less competent and faltering. This ability of the husbands to have energy and emotion available and to be significantly involved with their wives and children despite heavy investment in their work was striking.

Although this pattern of marital relationship was clear and seen in the parents of all the healthy families studied, the marital styles differed from couple to couple. Some had a more active, searching quality—an air of expectant electricity in the relationship. Life was exciting and somewhat unpredictable—the attitude was that of going out to meet it. Other couples, however, were quieter and were described by one of the research team as "like a powerful automobile idling." "Let's see what life brings" is more descriptive of this group than the searching attitude of the first group.

Cuber and Harroff have described five marital styles: devitalized, passive-congenial, conflict-habituated, vital, and total.* The devitalized marriage once was emotionally charged, but is no longer. The juice or spark is gone. The passive-congenial never had a charge, and the marriage seemed based from the start on something other than strong feelings. The conflict-habituated couples seem to get gratification out of harpooning each other, and the endless conflicts appear to be the cement that binds them together. The vital and total marriages represent strongly charged relationships. None of the healthy families we studied had parental relationships that could be described as devitalized, passive-congenial, or conflict-habituated. They were, at the minimum, vital. The "connection" between husband and wife was strong, but it was not at the expense of either partner's individuality. These men and women had their own thoughts, ideas, and feelings.

There was obvious complementarity in these relationships. The husband and wife seemed to "fit" together well. If a husband had any tendency towards strong-handedness, the wife was skillful at helping him to modulate this. If the wife was a big talker, the husband appeared quietly thoughtful.

It certainly is not my intention to present a picture of problem-free or "perfect" relationships. There were conflicts; compromises were not always easy to reach; and, on occasions, solutions were labored. Most of the time, however, these couples were very effective in communicating with each other, and that clarity allowed the early identification of problems. Their skill in negotiation appeared to account for the absence of underlying smoldering, chronic disagreements or problems. As a consequence, the mood that prevailed most times within the relationship was warm and caring.

---

*Cuber, John F., and Harroff, Peggy B. *The Significant Americans.* Appleton-Century, New York, 1965.

IN BED

Sex serves many purposes within a relationship. Sex can be a period of deepest intimacy, an interlude of sensuous play, the periodic enactment of a dominant-submissive theme, a recommitment of the partners to each other and their shared future, an imposition, a duty, a lusty screwing, a coming together in which touching and holding are more important than intercourse, a joyous hello, or a tender parting —and more. To complicate the matter further, on any single occasion, sex is often a combination of several of these themes, and that which is of greatest importance to one partner may be of little importance to the other partner.

For these reasons, the studies that deal only with frequency of intercourse and degree of satisfaction, important as they are, fail to present a full picture. In fact, the studies may not get at what is most important about sex for a particular couple. Understanding the issues underlying sex for a particular couple is difficult and requires a type of study in which the researcher and the subject or subjects explore together topics of which the subjects may not be initially aware. One can only rarely do so in a brief interview or by using a questionnaire.

With this sense of the incompleteness about what we know about sex in mind, let us turn to a consideration of that which is reasonably clear. The first fact is that, when interviewed privately, individuals and their spouses often report different intercourse frequencies. These differences are so striking that the interviewer often wonders if the couple live in the same world.

> *Interviewer*: "How often do you have intercourse?"
> *Wife*: "Well, that varies from time to time. More often on vacation trips out of town ... but ... probably on the average of three to four times a week."
> *Husband*: (in a separate, private interview) "Well, let's see ... it's different at different times ... but week after week ... I'd say once every ten days."

This type of difference occurs in people who seem well oriented and in no way "out of it." Nevertheless, in this specific area each reports such a different view of the frequency of their sex as to suggest that there is something very wrong with the sexual relationship for one or (more likely) both partners. Specifically, if one partner feels that intercourse is too frequent and the other partner feels it is not often enough, there is a strong likelihood that they will count differently.

Although reporting different frequencies by the partners suggests the presence of problems, privately many couples report identical frequencies, but this fact, by itself, does not necessarily indicate the absence of problems.

A second aspect of the available information regarding the frequency of intercourse is that for any group of couples of approximately the same age and background there will be wide variations from couple to couple in the reported frequency of intercourse. In those couples in which the partners report the same frequency, one finds frequencies that range from once every month or so to five or more times each week.

It is necessary to add a second factor to our understanding: the degree of sexual satisfaction experienced by each partner. In this regard, it is important to distinguish between orgasm and sexual satisfaction; they are not always the same.

"Well, I almost always have an orgasm . . . Jack is . . . well, technically, I guess a good lover . . . but, more often than not I'm left with the feeling that something is missing. I don't know what it is . . . maybe, to put it bluntly, we screw good . . . but we're often not together in some emotional way."

"I don't know exactly how to put it . . . it's good sex . . . Jane usually has an orgasm and I ejaculate . . . from that viewpoint all goes well . . . but somehow it's not as good or exciting . . . it doesn't seem to mean that much anymore. I don't know if it's me . . . or us . . . or what the deal is . . . but the sense of real satisfaction is missing."

"Harold is not really that much of a lover boy. More often than not, I don't reach a climax . . . but somehow it's almost always good. It's the being together, the holding each other, sometimes the laughs we share about how awkward the deal is . . . It's a very satisfying part of our relationship."

"Well, it really is strange. Neither of us are red hot in bed. I tend to ejaculate prematurely, and Edith is kind of frigid . . . oh, once in a while we get it all together and everything happens like the books say . . . but even when it doesn't go well . . . physically that is . . . we . . . a . . . help each other and . . . well, it's . . . a . . . very satisfying . . . I think for both of us."

These descriptions illustrate the fact that orgasm is not necessarily associated with high levels of satisfaction, and that high levels of satisfaction can occur in the absence of orgasm. For many couples, however, there is a correlation between orgasm and high levels of satisfaction. The point is that for some couples there can be one without the other, and the two should not be considered as necessarily the same.

The frequency of intercourse and level of sexual satisfaction may reflect a wide variety of nonsexual aspects both of the couple's relationship and of their individual personalities. Sexual therapists have come to realize that, for some couples, a disturbance in their sex life may cause many difficulties in all other aspects of the relationship. In other couples, however, the very same sexual disturbance is more the result of other difficulties than it is the cause.

Clifford Sager, a respected leader in the field of couples therapy, has suggested that the concept of marriage contracts is a useful way to understand a marriage.* By marriage contracts, Sager refers to both expressed and unexpressed expectations each partner brings to the relationship. Together these individual expectations go into the formation of an interactional contract—that set of unspoken rules and tactics the couple evolves in the effort to meet each spouse's individual needs. Each spouse has sexual expectations, and together the couple evolves a sexual component to their joint contract. This will include such issues as what attracts them sexually, how they like to have sex initiated, what forms of sexual activity will be involved, what is to be the frequency of intercourse, how sex may vary at different times, and many others. Nevertheless, it is important to keep in mind that the sexual aspects of the relationship can be understood only as one part of the total relationship. Let me illustrate the importance of this with the following case histories.

---

* Sager, Clifford J. *Marriage Contracts and Couple Therapy*. Brunner/Mazel, New York, 1976.

"Good" Sex in a Bad Relationship

Harold and Sue Smith were seen together as one part of the clinical evaluation of Harold's growing dependence on alcohol. Their relationship was clearly a conflicted, dominant-submissive one. Sue, a successful educator, was the more aggressive partner and, in joint interviews, interrupted Harold and was openly derisive. Harold, a quiet and somewhat passive skilled worker, seemed in awe of his wife and her success. He denied being angry about her dominant behavior, and seemed unaware that his excessive drinking was one of the few aspects of their life together that she was unable to control. During the months preceding the evaluation, Sue had become increasingly rageful at Harold, and his drinking had increased.

In discussing their sex life with them, it became apparent that this was one of the strengths of their relationship. The pattern of their sex started with Sue's signal that she wanted intercourse. She did this by wearing a certain gown. Harold always responded to this signal and, permission having been granted, then became the sexual aggressor. Sue did not need to control sexual foreplay or intercourse beyond being the only one who could decide when sex was to occur. They both described what can be termed mechanically good sex. Orgasms were the rule, and they both said that the sex was highly satisfactory.

"Good" and "bad" are, of course, relative terms. Although the Smiths experienced their sexual relationship as a "good" part of their relationship—it usually resulted in orgasms and each felt it was satisfying—another couple with a different type of relationship might find it seriously deficient. They would point out its sameness or rigid patterning, the lack of any sense of joy or play, and the apparent lack of emotional intimacy. Contrast it, for example, with this report from another couple.

"Good" Sex in a Good Relationship

Helen and Marty Jones were studied as part of a research investigation of family life. Their relationship was one of shared power. Marty, an electronics engineer, was successful in his work and received frequent promotions. Helen was not employed outside the home but, in addition to her responsibilities for the children and home, was involved in a number of civic groups. Helen and Marty made most decisions together. At

times, they disagreed, and each searched for an effective compromise. Each had areas of particular strength and provided the
family with leadership in these areas.

In discussing their sexual relationship, both indicated a high
level of satisfaction. Either could, and did, initiate sex. "It depends on who is more in the mood." They both described a
variety of different "kinds" of sex. "Often, it's serious, very
close—lots of very private talk—but, at other times, it's more
playful—like how many different ways can each find to turn the
other one on the most—lots of laughing and fun. Once in a while,
it's just very horny—just really going after each other tooth and
nail." Each of them described their sex life as usually resulting in
orgasm and highly satisfactory.

Helen and Marty would find Harold and Sue's kind of sexual relationship sadly deficient—it likely would seem stereotyped and restric-
tive. When considered, however, within the overall relationships
established by Harold and Sue, it was a "good" part of their relationship, and each seemed to be sincere when describing it as satisfactory.

There is, then, a need to understand a couple's sexual life beyond
the simple responses to questions having to do with frequency, orgasm, and satisfaction. It must be considered within the context of
their total relationship. It can be one of the few strengths in a troubled
relationship, a relatively unimportant part of a good relationship—
any number of combinations are possible—but, more often than not,
there is "good" sex in a "good" relationship, and "bad" or highly
unsatisfactory sex in a troubled relationship.

In the healthy families studied, the parents' sexual relationship was
very gratifying to both husband and wife. The frequency of sexual
intercourse varied from couple to couple, with some very active
(three to five times per week), and others relatively inactive (one to
two times per month). In private interviews, husband and wife
reported identical frequencies. Levels of sexual satisfaction were
reported as very high. Orgasm was the rule, but what was even more
impressive was the way in which these individuals discussed the fact
that sexual satisfaction involved the gratification of a variety of needs
—to feel close, to touch, to be held.

The following description may give the flavor of one type of marriage found in the study of healthy families.

Carl and Holly Storch volunteered to participate in a research study of family life. They were both in their early forties and had been married 19 years. Their three daughters were 16, 13, and 11. Carl was an assistant principal of an inner-city high school, and Holly was a substitute teacher, working on the average of two days a week. They lived in the suburbs in a three-bedroom, 14-year-old house.

Carl was the oldest of three siblings of a farming family. He was quiet and self-disciplined, but he related to others with obvious warmth. Holly, the younger daughter of a small business-man, was more outgoing with strangers. She had an infectious sense of humor and seemed less firmly self-disciplined.

Carl and Holly met during their sophomore year at college, went steady for two years, and married immediately following graduation. They both taught school until the birth of their first child. Shortly thereafter, Carl started graduate school during the summers and, after several years, received his graduate degree. Holly returned to substitute teaching when their youngest daughter entered kindergarten. Their life together was pat-terned around teaching, their activities with their daughters, the care of their home and yard, and a shared interest in literature and classical music. Holly played bridge each week with friends, and Carl played poker for small stakes with a group of neighbor-hood men several times a month.

In individual, exploratory interviews, both were open and discussed a wide variety of personal matters with apparent candor.

Carl mentioned no significant symptoms—describing himself as "rather a level person without strong highs or lows." He dis-cussed what seemed to be a normal grief reaction to the death of his parents in an automobile accident several years earlier. He described his relationship with Holly as the closest he had ever experienced. He felt he could be completely open with her and could not recall any subject or feeling he was unable to discuss with her. He did not smoke, enjoyed a beer when he got home from work, and did not use medication other than an occasional aspirin for headache or muscular soreness. Carl had never had a serious illness, fracture, or surgical procedure.

Holly also denied any symptoms. She felt "a little tense" a few days prior to some of her menstrual periods, but took no medication. She expressed concern for her widowed mother who lived alone, and indicated that she and Carl had discussed the fact that the time might come when she would be unable to live alone. She thought they would ask her to move in with them, and indicated that she had more questions about the wisdom of that arrangement than did Carl.

Holly discussed a period during late adolescence when she felt confused and depressed. The family physician had recommended a psychiatrist, and she had four or five helpful sessions with him. She felt she had learned that at the root of her distress was anxiety about leaving home for college. She considered herself a healthy and strong person, but maybe a "little too dependent on Carl—he is so solid." She was seen by the interviewer as an open, warm woman without significant problems.

Independent judgments based on transcripts of these interviews placed both Carl and Holly in the healthy level of psychological functioning.

When interviewed together and during a marital problem-solving test, the observers made the following comments:

"This couple relates with openness and obvious warmth. There is an easygoing and casual mood to their discussions. When confronted with differences of opinion, they expressed surprise. 'I didn't know you really felt that way!' They quickly clarified their difference of opinion, bantered good-naturedly, and soon reached a compromise. On another difference revealed to them, they failed to reach a compromise, and agreed to differ. There was no competitive undercurrent. They seemed to share power and, although at times Holly appeared to verge on deferring to Carl's judgment, in the final analysis she does not, nor does Carl try to impose his views upon her. During the marital testing, they maintain eye contact and touch each other frequently."

Both described their sexual relationship as highly satisfying. They had intercourse about twice a week, and both consistently achieved orgasm. Each indicated in the private interview that they were still "turned on" by the other. Sex included considerable foreplay and often a good deal of "pillow talk." They both enjoyed sleeping nude, and for some years had locked their bedroom door at night. On their occasional trips out of town, they enjoyed staying at hotels where "soft pornography" films were available on television. "I'm perhaps a little more adventurous sexually than Carl—sometimes I'll suggest something new—even a little kinky once in a while. He invariably ends up liking it, though. It's really a very free kind of way of being with each other."

There had been no major traumas in their life. The only real crisis was the recent death of Carl's parents. Holly said that there were occasions when she regretted not having a son—"Carl is such a man's man—he's great with boys—and I don't want him to miss anything. When I mention it to him, he smiles and says that he has sneaky female sperm or that he enjoys the lack of competition or something like that—I've come to feel it really doesn't bother him—maybe it's me who kind of wants everything perfect."

They see three or four couples with some regularity. "Usually dinner together—once in a while we all sail with the Fenders or play some tennis with the Cohens. Mostly though, it's dinner and talk." Both Holly and Carl feel that their only significant extravagance is "good" season seats at the symphony.

Carl is an expert home repairman, the more athletic of the two, and a better card player. Holly writes the checks and is more knowledgeable about the small investments they are able to make. Carl's share of his parents' modest estate has been put aside for the girls' education, and they both sense this with a "real relief." They go to church occasionally and both profess a belief in God, although Holly's God is in the image of a loving person, and Carl's God is more a "central organizing force in nature."

The Storches are representative of a kind of marriage found in healthy families. Other healthy couples may have a vastly different style—more active or charged, for example, but the underlying shared power, mutual respect, open communication, capacity for intimacy, and highly satisfactory sex are the similarities that lie beneath the differing styles. The Storches "fit" well together. They genuinely like each other and remain obviously in love.

The impact of this type of relationship on the family as a whole will be evident as our focus turns to the family. What is apparent, however, is that couples like Carl and Holly are fortunate. They have constructed a relationship that offers each of them a sense of closeness, security, and meaning. In evolving this type of marriage, they provide themselves with the opportunity for continued growth as well as a bulwark against life's stresses.

IV

Looking at the Whole Family

Most people think about others only as individuals. It is common, for example, to think about the Smith family as Bill Smith, his wife, Ann, and their two children, Chuck and Karen. In thinking about them, many people would think only about their individual characteristics. Bill is 33, an electronics technician, tall, thin, and very quiet. Ann is 29, works at a local bank, is short, pretty, and very outgoing. Chuck, at nine, is quiet and studious, while Karen is unusually outgoing for a five-year-old. All of these observations are about the individuals in the Smith family and, although they may be accurate, tell us little about the Smiths as a family.

To underscore this point, let us construct two Smith families, each containing four individuals who fit the above descriptions but emphasizing the differences in the families those four persons could belong to.

Smith Family #1

Dinnertime is a pleasant, warm experience. Ann talks more than Bill, but he participates in discussions in a thoughtful, humorous way. The children are spontaneous and take part in the conversation. All four listen to each other and approach differences as matters of interest and variety or as situations on which they can reach a compromise. If Chuck and Karen argue, one of the parents moves rapidly but gently to clarify the basic issue and help resolve the problem. When the meal is over,

40

everyone helps clear the table. Often, Bill gives Ann a hug or kiss as they are cleaning up. There is a real sense that all the members of the family enjoy being together.

Smith Family #2

Dinnertime is usually a tense, unenjoyable event. Ann does most of the talking, and a good deal of it is critical. She zeros in on the children's table manners or openly criticizes the way Bill takes care of the yard or makes household repairs. He seldom responds directly, but retreats in a sullen, detached way. Occasionally, Chuck and Karen try to talk with each other and are ignored by the parents unless they are quarreling, which may result in their being sent to their rooms. The meal ends with Ann's assigning various chores to each. Together they seem sulky, unpleasant, and trapped.

If the mealtime observations of these two Smith families are more-or-less typical for each—if they represent a basic pattern of family life rather than an unusual response—life within the two families is very different for the two Anns, Bills, and their children. On the surface, the individuals may appear alike, but the basic family patterns are remarkably different. Growing up or living in such dissimilar families may result in profound differences in every aspect of each individual's life. To understand the many ways in which family characteristics differ and influence the lives of the family members, one must be able to observe the characteristics of the whole family.

Part of the difficulty in shifting our view from the individual to the family as a whole is that we are accustomed to examining and trying to understand behavior only in terms of the individual. Even our vocabulary, which offers a wealth of words that describe individual behavior (for example, shy, aggressive, insecure, impulsive, friendly, suspicious), has few words that tell us what goes on between people. Also, we cherish the rights of the individual and place them high on our list of values, as reflected in our laws. There are fewer laws that address the rights of the family.

Although the idea that a family is more than a group of individuals has been around for a good while, most studies of family life have involved observing the individuals in a family and making a composite to describe the family. Only recently have families been studied as a unit, more than the simple sum of the personality traits and values of the individual members—a system that has characteristics of its own. The characteristics of the family as a system can be understood only by using techniques that are appropriate to the study of the whole family.

The family system approach to studying a family focuses on "how" a family relates, communicates, and solves problems, rather than relying only on "what" family members will or can tell one about their family. The important feature of this approach is to present the family with something to discuss—a problem to solve, for example—and then measure how the family discusses and solves the problem. One observes various aspects of the family as a communication system. Examples of what one observes include who controls, dominates, or leads the discussion, the clarity of family members' messages to each other, the pattern of interruptions within the family, the amount of conflict, the efficiency of the family in solving the problem presented to them, and a number of other aspects of their family discussion.

An important feature of this approach is that while the family members are aware that they are being observed or measured, and they may be cautious about "what" they say, they often have little awareness of either "how" they communicate with each other or that the process, rather than the content, is being evaluated.

This approach to studying the family is based upon a small group of assumptions. These include:

1) The family, as a system, is more than the sum of its parts. This deceptively simple notion addresses itself to what can be called the "emergent" qualities of the family—those characteristics of the family that cannot be understood by simply adding the family members' individual personalities, characteristics, or values. The biologist, Lewis Thomas, was dealing with this feature of social groups when he described certain aspects of the behavior of ants.* He pointed out that an ant has a simple brain, and there is no way such a brain can be considered to have ideas. It is not complex enough. However, if one watches five or six ants work together to get a dead moth to an ant-

---

* Thomas, Lewis. *The Lives of a Cell.* Viking Press, New York, 1974.

hill, it is impossible to understand their behavior as simply five or six simple brains added together. Some features larger than the sum emerge.

In a similar way, marital intelligence has been studied.* A couple may take an intelligence test together, and the results may yield a higher joint intelligence than either the husband or wife has individually! Once again, something unpredictable from the study of the individual emerges in the interactions between individuals.

2) The family as a system develops patterns of response. The family, starting with the parents' courtship and marriage, evolves certain ways of dealing with day-to-day life. Some of these patterns are obvious to all—who cooks, washes dishes, feeds the pets, bathes the children, and many more. Others, however, are less apparent to the casual observer. They include who has the right to make what decisions, how differences of opinion are to be handled, whether or not affection, anger, or other feelings can be expressed openly, and a host of other important aspects of living in a family.

The development of family patterns is necessary in order to deal with all the things that a family must face, decide, and accomplish in daily life. If some type of stable pattern did not evolve, the result would be a chaotic existence, a form of anarchy.

It is important to emphasize that these less apparent patterns, so central to family life, may operate outside of family members' awareness. Some, of course, are clear to all; others would be quickly recognized if family members were asked about them; still, the presence of some is not known to the family.

3) Some family patterns are constructive and others destructive. Skynner has said that it should come as no surprise that the family, with its tremendous capacity for creativity, including that of life itself, should have also a remarkable capacity for destruction.** It is the patterns of relationships within the family that determine whether or not the family will accomplish the two tasks of being a family:

---

* Roman, M., and Bauman, G. Interaction testing. In: Harrower, Vorbaus, Roman, and Bauman, *Creative Variations in the Projective Techniques.* Charles C Thomas, Springfield, Ill., 1960.

** Skynner, A. C. R. *Systems of Family and Marital Psychotherapy.* Brunner/Mazel, New York, 1976.

stabilization of the parents' personalities and the production of auto-nomous children. Some patterns of relationships accomplish these two tasks very well; others fail and result in psychiatric disturbances, in-complete maturation of children and, ultimately, disintegration of the family unit. It is with this understanding that a continuum of family competence can be constructed. The continuum (Figure 1) is a simple representation of how well families accomplish the two basic jobs of the family.

Healthy families encourage the continued growth of the parents' personalities and raise healthy, autonomous children. Faltering families raise healthy, autonomous children, but do not encourage further growth for the parents and, in fact, may strain the personality of one or both parents. Troubled families fail to accomplish one or both of these tasks, and severely troubled families fail at both.

The research study of families on which this continuum is based included a number of procedures selected in order to reach as clear an understanding of each family as possible. A central part of the research was the study of how the family communicates—that is, the communication patterns each family had evolved over time. Examples may illustrate this newer way of studying the family. If, for example, you ask family members how they solve family problems, the most common response is, "We talk about them and either agree or reach some compromise." If you next ask each family member to write an

Figure 1

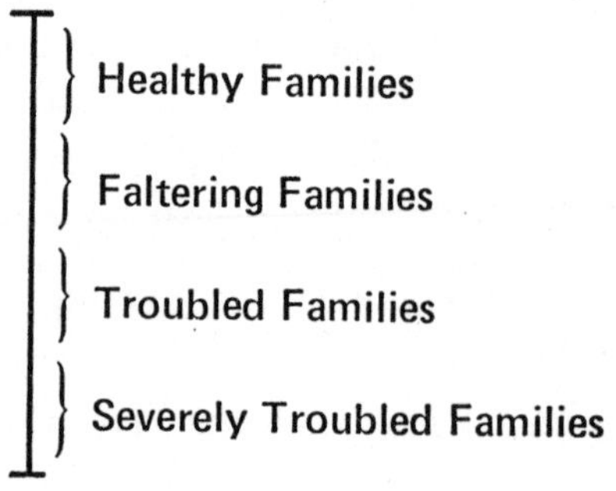

Healthy Families

Faltering Families

Troubled Families

Severely Troubled Families

answer to the question, "What is the main problem in the family?",
collect the answers, inform the family that they disagree as to what
the main problem is, and ask them to discuss and solve their disagreement, you may see an approach to problem-solving very different
from what they said they do.

The Harts, for example, said that they discussed problems and
either agreed or found a compromise. Their individual, written answers to the "What is the main problem" question were:

> *Father*: "We spend too much money foolishly."
> *Mother*: "We don't communicate well."
> *Daughter*: "They are too strict about car dates."
> *Son*: "You can't watch televised ballgames on school nights."

When confronted with the fact that, as a family, they disagreed
about the main problem in their family, the following conversation
ensued:

> *Father*: "There is no question in my mind about the main prob-
> lem. What did you put down, Jack?
> *Son*: "Uh . . . well . . ."
> *Father*: "Speak up."
> *Son*: "You ought to be able to watch some ballgames."
> *Father*: "That's all you want to do—you do it on the weekends
> —but it's out on school nights. Your grades aren't perfect.
> That really is not a problem. What did you put down,
> Shirley?"
> *Daughter*: "Well . . . you know . . . the thing about car dates."
> *Father*: "What do you mean?"
> *Daughter*: "All my friends go out . . ."
> *Father*: "Damn! You know how little that means to me. I just
> don't see that as a problem. The rule is clear—you can car
> date when you're 16 and not until. What did you put down,
> honey?"
> *Mother*: "Communication."
> *Father*: "Communication?"
> *Mother*: "Yes."
> *Father*: "What does that mean?"
> *Mother*: "It could be better."
> *Father*: "How could it be better?"
> *Mother*: "Well . . . sometimes it's hard to get your point across."

Father: "In what way?"
Mother: "Well ... I don't ... it's hard to be specific ... but
once in a while ... well, you're very strong ... have firm
opinions ..."
Father: "What's wrong with that?"
Mother: "Well ... it's a ... a ... nothing really."
Father: "OK, then, we're agreed. Now we've got to do something about the money we spend. That's the problem—we
buy things we don't need and ... we must find a way to
stop.

In this example, a very dominant father completely controlled the
family conversation. He did so by taking charge, asking specific
questions, disregarding other family members' answers to the research question and, in general, running roughshod over the others
to support his own initial position. This pattern of a family dominated
by one member with the others submitting passively is very clear
when you see the family as a system. It might be apparent if you
talked with the individuals privately, but its demonstration by the
entire family is clear and does not leave the observer with the
dilemma of whom to believe.

In another exploratory task, a different family was asked to write
individually their answers to the question, "Who is the real boss in
your family?" Their answers were as follows:

Mother: "Father."
Father: "Father."
Daughter #1: "Father."
Daughter #2: "Father."

They were then asked to plan a family vacation together. One part
of their response was the following dialogue:

Father: "Well, we might go to ..."
Daughter #1: "California—to Disneyland!"
Mother: "That may be too far—what about Colorado?"
Father: "I was wondering ..."
Daughter #2: "I'd rather go to the beach. We could learn to
surf."
Mother: "That's not a bad idea. Why don't you express an
opinion, dear?"

Father: "I thought we could go see my parents and maybe spend some time . . ."
Mother: "Oh, we did that last year—let's just have a fun trip this time."
Daughter #1: "I vote for Disneyland!"
Daughter #2: "The beach!"
Mother: "How shall we decide?"
Father: "Maybe we could . . ."
Daughter #1: "Flip a coin!"

In this example, the family repeatedly interrupts the "real boss," Father, whenever he attempts to express an opinion. He appears to tolerate this disrespect and plods along. Whatever factors influence the development and consequences of this pattern, it does not appear consistent with their individual designations of Father as the "real boss" in the family. To the contrary, he appears to be the least influential member of the family. This finding came to the surface by focusing on "how" the family communicates rather than "what" they were able or willing to say about the subject.

The continuum of family competence raises an important question: What accounts for the differences among families located on different points of the continuum? The research study of families ranging from the healthy to the severely troubled highlights the complexity of answers to this question. There is no one factor so strong that it, alone, determines whether or not a family is healthy. We all search for simple answers to complex questions, and the question of what accounts for family health is no exception. People have suggested that "love," "belief in God," "strict discipline," "country living," "good nutrition," or any number of other single factors are the key to family health. The research fails to support this idea. Having a healthy family is *not* like getting the brass ring on the merrygo-round, and having a troubled family is *not* like getting the black bean in a drawing. Rather, a number of factors work together in determining how competent a family is. What, then, are these factors?

1) *The nature of the parents' relationship.* As described in Chapters II and III, a number of factors are involved in producing the type of marriage the parents have. These include the way the couple

settles how much power or influence each will have, the levels of communication of which they are capable, the quality and intensity of each spouse's alliances with others, the emotional "charge" in their relationship, how well their personalities "fit" together, how they deal with conflict, and the quality of their sexual relationship.

2) *The way the family deals with power.* This factor, as well as those which follow, is described in subsequent chapters. The family, taking its lead from the parents and their relationship, evolves a typical and easily recognizable pattern. Power may be shared, with the parents providing leadership, or one person may dominate. In other families, there is never-ending conflict about power and, for a few families, there is no stable pattern and chaos results.

3) *The amount and type of family closeness.* The crucial issue here is whether the family promotes high levels of *both* closeness and individuality.

4) *The way the family talks together.* A number of factors produce a family's pattern of communication. These include how much the family encourages clear communication, the taking of responsibility for individual feelings, thoughts, and actions, acknowledging each other's messages, talking with high levels of spontaneity, and allowing family members to speak for themselves.

5) *The way the family solves problems.* The central issue regarding family problem-solving is the extent to which the family relies on the process of negotiation and is efficient in its approach to problems.

6) *The way the family deals with feelings.* Each family evolves a pattern which determines how openly feelings may be expressed, the range of feelings that may be expressed, whether or not the expression of feelings leads to an empathic response, and the basic family mood when stress or crisis is not present.

7) *The ability of the family to accept and deal with change and loss.* Each family must come to grips with ever-present changes—both in the world around the family and within the family itself. Loss of loved ones, in particular, is a stressful change that families

must struggle with and accommodate to, in ways that either assist the mourning or delay it with unfortunate consequences.

8) *The values of the family.* Although often not openly discussed, each family reacts to life's challenges in accord with shared beliefs. These beliefs are the answers to basic questions such as "What is the nature of man?" and "What is the meaning of life?"

9) *The family's capacity for intimacy and autonomy.* These two issues can be seen as the family's crucial role in encouraging both autonomy and the capacity for intimacy in its members. Without both capabilities, individual family members are unable to participate fully in life.

These nine factors are associated closely with the family's overall level of competence or health. If one looks at a particular family and determines how the family deals with each of the nine factors, one can arrive at a reliable measure of where that family falls on the continuum of family competence. The patterns present in each of these nine areas determine whether the family is healthy, faltering, troubled, or severely troubled.

Let us retrace our steps briefly. Starting with a value judgment about the two key tasks of the family—stabilizing the parental personalities and raising autonomous children—a continuum was constructed. The continuum is a way to represent how well or how poorly a particular family accomplishes these two tasks. Families at various levels of competence have been studied, and nine aspects of family life account for the differences between families at various points on the continuum. The nine factors are, in themselves, complex, but do give us a useful handle on the measurement of family health.

Throughout the remainder of the book, these nine factors will be described. A major emphasis will be on what we learned from studying healthy families. Understanding what healthy families are like gives us a yardstick against which one's own family may be seen. More than that, however, the study of healthy families reveals something of what is possible in human relationships.

V

How the Family

Communicates

It is surprising how much can be learned from the way family members talk with each other. In fact, if one wishes to understand as much as possible about a family and has only a single source of information, a tape recording of a family's unrehearsed conversation would be valuable. The key is to concentrate on "how" the family communicates rather than "what" family members say. This distinction is important because most people pay attention only to what is being said. Listening to what people say, or "content attention," provides information, but, if one's goal is to learn as much as possible about a family, it is not as useful as listening to *how* a family communicates. Observing the way family members talk with each other can be called "process attention" because it focuses on the communication patterns that are typical for a family. The importance of this distinction may be appreciated in contrasting the following family conversations.

Family A

Mother: "Where are we going on our vacation this year?"
Father: "To St. Louis to see my parents."
Son: "I thought we were going to the beach."

50

Father: "Changed our plans—Grandmother is not feeling well."
Son: "Couldn't we go to the beach anyway?"
Father: "No."
Mother: "Perhaps we could, John . . ."
Father: "There's no way—I don't have the time or money for both."
Mother: "I guess that settles that."

Family B

Mother: "Where are we going on our vacation this year?"
Son: "To the beach! Don't you remember we talked about it last year?"
Father: "Well—we did—but we've got a problem. Grandmother isn't feeling well and wants us to come to St. Louis."
Mother: "That makes it a tough decision."
Son: "I really was looking forward to the beach—fishing, surfing, and all that.
Father: "I was too—but I'm sort of torn between what I want to do and what I think we ought to do."
Mother: "Is there any way to do both?"
Father: "I don't see how—I can only take a week, and the money is a problem . . ."
Son: "Do you think she's really sick?"
Father: "I'm afraid so . . ."
Mother: "I guess we'd better go to St. Louis."
Son: "Yeah . . ."
Father: "I feel bad about the disappointment."
Mother: "It really can't be helped."
Son: "Maybe next year, Dad."

If these brief family conversations are examined only from the viewpoint of their content—the "what" of communication—they are very much alike. Both families were discussing vacation plans and decided to go to St. Louis to visit a sick grandmother. The "how" of their exchange was very different, and it illuminates the way family members operate as a unit. In Family A, the decision came from Father, and his mind seemed made up. If he had any regrets or conflict about the vacation, they were not apparent. He paid no attention to the views of Mother or Son. Althuogh such domination may be efficient in reaching a decision quickly, it precludes any serious consideration of the thoughts and feelings of the other

members who will be affected by it. (And one might speculate that
his brusqueness covers his pain and resentment of having to be the
"bad guy.")

Family B reached the same conclusion—they, too, were going to
St. Louis to see Grandmother—but the process of their talking together was very different from Family A's. Father shared his inner
conflict about what he wanted to do and what he felt they ought to
do. He did not impose a ready-made decision on the family. As a
consequence, the mother and son were able to participate in the
decision—it was a shared choice. This can have important consequences. Everyone in Family B can feel that his or her feelings and
thoughts were important and were taken into consideration. Both the
disappointment of missing the beach vacation and the concern about
Grandmother were shared. Another ramification of this way of
solving problems together is that father shares the responsibility for
the decision and, therefore, need not feel that he is the one who
deprives the others. For him, their participation may mean that he
feels less alone in his own family. Also, Mother and Son, having
helped to make the decision, were less likely to feel deprived and
angry. If both families drive to St. Louis, the mood in Family B's
car is apt to be very different from that in Family A's car.

To draw any conclusions about the two families from such brief
conversations is to presume that the pattern of each family's communications was typical for them. Research has shown that families
do evolve a typical way of communicating, relating, and solving
problems, perhaps because it would be impossible to evolve a new
approach to every situation or problem. To have to do so would
overwhelm any family. It is through observing a family's typical
communication pattern that we can begin to grasp the workings of
the family. There are, of course, situations in which a family's
typical pattern of communication is not appropriate and is put aside
temporarily. A family that relies on sharing feelings and problems and
reaches solutions by negotiations in which all participate would certainly discard this approach if the family car were stalled on the
railroad tracks with a train approaching. They simply would not
take time to discuss everyone's opinion. One family member, probably a parent, would order everyone out of the car. There are such

situations in the lives of most families—perhaps, not stalled cars on the railroad tracks, but equally serious situations in which survival is threatened, and the family's usual way of operating must be put aside. While such situations (by their very character) are the exception, it is important to keep in mind when one is listening to "how" a family communicates that the circumstances in which the conversation occurs must always be considered.

In order to develop process attention, that is, a better "ear" for how a family communicates, one must pay attention to at least three major aspects of family communication. These are the family's approach to problem-solving, the style of family communication, and the way in which the family expresses and responds to feelings.

FAMILY PROBLEM-SOLVING

There are a few basic ways a family approaches problems, and most families appear to rely on one pattern primarily. These basic styles can be described as:

1) A family pattern of negotiation.
2) A family pattern of domination.
3) A family pattern of conflict.
4) A family pattern of denial.

In the first three patterns, the characterization concerns the way in which the family deals with power. The problem-solving pattern directly reflects the distribution of power within the family. In families in which power is shared rather than concentrated in one person, problems are approached in a way that allows each family member to have his or her say; each member's feelings and thoughts are considered important. Such a family develops a pattern of negotiation. In each situation or problem, any family member may be the one who leads, although usually in a family with young children it is one of the parents. Families using this pattern habitually deal with problems as they arise; they spend time making certain the problem is clearly defined and agreed upon; then they explore possible solutions. Because this pattern encourages all family members to participate, solutions are apt to be more creative. When there is general agreement on the best answer, that is accepted as the solution. If there is not general agreement within the family, a compromise is sought. On those occasions where neither agreement nor compromise can be reached, the family agrees to disagree and, most often, one or both parents make the decision. The conversation of Family B exemplifies a family pattern of negotiation. Its distinguishing features are the respect it offers the feelings and opinions of each member and the shared responsibility for solutions.

Family A's conversation reflects a family pattern of domination. In this pattern, one person has a much more powerful position than other family members, and uses his or her power to dominate and control the family. He or she may do so openly—that is, with "raw power"—or with considerable finesse—that is, with "hidden power." In a family dominated by one individual's raw power, there is little to suggest that the powerful person has any real concern for what others feel or think. The dominant one makes all the decisions and is rarely influenced by opinions or feelings of other family members. In a family dominated by an individual with hidden power, the pattern is more subtle, but the individual does control. The techniques of hidden power revolve around the dominant one's control of what is discussed by the family. He or she may do this by asking questions, changing the subject, failing to answer questions that make his or her position on a problem appear questionable, or by ending discussions prematurely. In some families, this style of domination is obvious, but in others it can be such a smooth technique that its essential controllingness is not easily comprehended.

The pattern of domination presents difficulties for everyone in the family. The powerless members often come to feel "one-down," and may doubt their own importance, fail to develop self-confidence and, as a consequence, experience mounting resentment of the dominant one. Since direct verbal attacks are dangerous in a family with a pattern of dominance, indirect expression of anger is more frequent —forgetting something important to the powerful one, behavior disturbances in school or neighborhood, or any one of hundreds of ways of indirect rebellion. The dominant person also suffers. He or she may come to feel overwhelmed by having the responsibility for all decisions, and the anger of the others may lead to a feeling of being all alone. Loneliness is painful under all circumstances, but it can be particularly difficult when it occurs within one's family where one hopes to experience the greatest sense of connectedness with others.

The family pattern of conflict in problem-solving is suggested in the following brief family conversation.

Family C

> *Mother*: "When are we going to the beach for our vacation?"
> *Father*: "We're not—we're going to St. Louis . . ."
> *Mother*: "What do you mean we're not?"
> *Father*: "Just what I said."
> *Son*: "We agreed to go . . ."
> *Father*: "We can't—Grandmother is sick."
> *Mother*: "She's always sick."
> *Father*: "Why don't you get off her back?"
> *Mother*: "Why don't you get off her lap!"
> *Father*: "Oh—shut up!"
> *Mother*: "Who do you think you are—you can't tell me to shut up."
> *Father*: "I just did."
> *Son*: "Gee—do we have to . . ."
> *Mother*: "Stay out of this, Johnnie—it's not your business."
> *Father*: "That's right."

In this pattern, the presence of underlying, unsolved relationship problems consistently interferes with attempts to deal with new difficulties. Most often, the fundamental interpersonal problems are between mother and father, and the presence of any new and real trouble serves as a stimulus to bring the relationship problem out into the open. The pattern of conflict is inefficient and destructive to all members of the family. Sometimes families with this style of communication "select" certain topics and fight about them repeatedly—the father's relationship with his parents, the son's school grades, or mother's cooking. It can be almost anything, but it usually avoids real issues—some type of basic disagreement in the marital relationship. The unfaced conflict sets the tone for each and every day of the family's life together. Families who are severely conflicted may come home only when they have nowhere else to go, for home offers little joy or sense of connectedness.

The family pattern of denial in problem-solving may be the most ruinous of all, for the family typically refuses to acknowledge the very existence of problems. The extent of this obliviousness can range from modest to severe, even to the point of a shared distortion of a painful reality. One sees families that contain a member with a severe psychiatric illness to which the family responds by acting as if the illness were not present. Once, in interviewing a family containing a severely disturbed 15-year-old son who heard voices, thought his teachers were planning to kill him, and carried a loaded pistol with him, I suggested to the family that he seemed to be very distressed and struggling with some painful feelings. They responded in this dialogue:

> *Mother*: "Oh, he's ... well, perhaps, a little tense ... but nothing serious."
> *Father*: "That's right, doctor, it may be that he isn't quite himself—but Owen will be fine, won't you, Owen?"
> *Owen*: "They're after me ... they say ... (inaudible) ... killing ... going to get me."
> *Mother*: "You see, doctor—perfectly alright—just needs, well, maybe a sedative, ... vitamins."
> *Father*: "That's why we're here—we know that there really isn't anything wrong, but the principal said Owen couldn't return to school without clearance, and our family doctor insisted that we see you."

This family dealt with the existence of a clearly apparent and serious disturbance in their son by denying that it existed. This is a particularly destructive pattern. In this example, the reality was too frightening for them to face, so Owen could not receive the help he desperately needed. Although many families may, on rare occasions, deny a reality that is painful, this family had adopted denial as a pattern in most problematic situations. Inescapable problems that are avoided for a long time become severe and very difficult, perhaps impossible, to resolve effectively.

Of the four basic ways families approach problems, two patterns usually result in a solution: the pattern of negotiation and the pattern of dominance. In the pattern of conflict, the family can seldom cooperate enough to arrive at an answer to a problem, and the family with a pattern of denial fails consistently.

STYLE OF FAMILY COMMUNICATION

Families differ also in regard to the characteristics that, in sum, comprise the way they talk together. There are a number of factors involved, but five important ones are clarity, responsibility, permeability, spontaneity, and invasiveness.

Some families communicate with high levels of clarity. Members express how they feel and what they think in unambiguous terms, and they have a high level of openness with each other. An observer of the family dialogue rarely asks, "I wonder what they meant by that?" It is easy to follow the sequence of ideas as family members talk. Other families, however, are very obscure, and the observer may feel either that the family is using some type of undecipherable shorthand or that the level of disorganization makes much of what they say hard to understand. Between these two extremes, there are families with intermediate levels of clarity.

Another factor that influences the family communication style is responsibility. To what degree does the family encourage or insist that members accept the responsibility for their own actions, thoughts, and feelings? Some families teach that one must be accountable, while other families evade, blur, or deny responsibility, or blame others for their own actions, thoughts, or feelings.

"The teacher flunked me."

"She started it—I was just standing there minding my own business."

"Anyone would drink under those circumstances."

"That's not what I said; your mother misunderstood."

"At least our yard looks better than our neighbor's."

Although there are circumstances under which each of those statements might reflect some reality, when a family consistently speaks in this way there is the flavor of evading personal responsibility and blaming others.

Permeability describes an openness to what others say and the willingness to acknowledge their messages. In many families, when any member speaks or gives some sign, the others respond—with words, a smile, a shrug—but the speaker knows that he or she has been heard and his or her message is acknowledged. If a family is impervious, it may have a very crushing impact upon the individual whose statements are ignored. Imagine how the six-year-old boy in this example must feel:

Family D

> *Mother*: "Then we went out, and when we came home . . ."
> *Son*: "Mama, can I have a coloring book?"
> *Mother*: ". . . and when we got there, we found her (points to 14-year-old daughter) with him . . . and, well . . . they were on the sofa and had no clothes . . ."
> *Son*: "Mama! The coloring book?"
> *Mother*: "Well, we hit the ceiling."
> *Father*: "It was bad, very bad—I ordered him out of . . ."
> *Son*: "The coloring book . . ."
> *Father*: ". . . the house and forbade her to ever see him again."
> *Mother*: "She's been grounded ever since."
> *Son*: "Mama, can I have the coloring book?"
> *Daughter*: "It's been six weeks now, and I think that's enough —don't you?" (looks at therapist)
> *Father*: "That's the issue—we feel she shouldn't be out at night . . . and . . ."
> *Son*: "The coloring book . . . I want the book." (starts to cry)
> *Mother*: "It's a matter of trust—we just can't trust her."

Not only did they ignore the son's statements, but no one looked at him, touched him, or in any way recognized that he was alive and present in the family. If this is a pattern rather than an isolated episode, it can readily be imagined that the youngster might wonder, "Who am I?" "Do I exist?" Such a process over time can have serious consequences for his developing sense of self.

Some families communicate very spontaneously. In the free-flowing, natural style of their conversation, interruptions are frequent and happen to everyone. Despite this level of spontaneity, meaning is clear. Other families, however, talk with little spontaneity. There is a formal, stilted quality to the conversation. A typewritten transcript of a family's conversation reveals that there are many completed sentences in contrast to a transcript of a spontaneous family, in which the rapid exchange doesn't permit many formally completed sentences.

Stilted Family Communication

Father: "Were shall we eat?"
Son: "I would like to go to the Chinese place."
Mother: "How about Mexican food?"
Daughter: "I think Chinese food might be good."
Mother: "What about you?" (looking at father)
Father: "I'll vote for Chinese food."
Mother: "I'm outvoted."

Spontaneous Family Communication

Father: "Where shall we eat?"
Son: "Chinese . . ."
Mother: "I vote for Mexican . . ."
Daughter: "Chinese for me—let's . . ."
Father: "Sounds like the decision is . . ."
Mother: "Chinese food!"

Some circumstances in family life call for a more deliberate and formal dialogue. This is particularly true when they must deal with situations of considerable gravity. There are, however, families with only one conversational gear—it is always formal, proper, and stilted. Such families are unable to shift to a more freewheeling verbal style. Their discussions are tightly controlled, regardless of the circumstances. Other families seem to select the style most appropriate to the moment, to interrupt each other, and do so without losing the meaning or direction of their exchange. One key to this tendency is the observation that everyone gets equal treatment rather than one family member getting cut off repeatedly. Of course, under different or more serious circumstances, spontaneous families may use a more formal style of talking.

Still another factor influencing a family's style of communication involves invasiveness. This is the tendency in some families for members to read the minds of other family members—to assume, for the moment, that they really know what each other is feeling or thinking.

> "John, go get an apple—you're hungry," rather than, "If you're hungry, get an apple, John."
>
> "Mary, you are angry with me," rather than, "I get the feeling, Mary, that you may be angry with me."
>
> "Harold—you're cold—close the door!" rather than, "Harold, are you cold?"
>
> "Mark, you really want to hurt me," rather than, "I'm hurt, Mark, when you act this way."

Each of these statements has a presumptive quality, as if one individual really knows what the other thinks or feels. In a sense, some of these examples confuse impact with intent. Rather than, "This is what I feel," the message is, "This is what you feel," or "Look at what you're doing to me."

In some families, the individuals invade each other frequently. In others it is rarely observed and, on those infrequent occasions when it does occur, the invader is apt to be repelled.

> *Mother*: (to six-year-old son) "Sammy, you're tired—why don't you take a nap?"
> *Son*: "No, I'm not tired, Mama."

DEALING WITH FEELINGS

Another important aspect of how a family communicates is the manner in which feelings are handled. This ranges from being unusually open with all feelings, to being open with certain feelings, to avoiding all feelings. Since feelings are such a significant part of life, each person must develop some way of dealing with them. Most individuals learn in the family in which they grow up to be either expressive or inhibited with their feelings. The developing child observes that the parents either express their emotions freely or hide them. If the family prohibits the expression of most feelings, the child is apt to feel that having any strong emotions is abnormal or bad.

Jane, the 17-year-old daughter of two physicians, had been witness all her life to both parents' conviction that all anger was bad or destructive. They never raised their voices, expressed irritation, scowled, or muttered—let alone openly expressed anger with each other. Jane's earliest memory was being spanked by her mother because she had hit at her older brother angrily. The spanking had been delivered "without anger—just matter-of-factly." Jane had developed into a shy, introverted adolescent who had few friends or social interests. She had been referred to a psychiatrist following a nearly successful suicide attempt. After a number of interviews, it became clear that Jane experienced considerable rage; behind her shyness was a time bomb of anger. She had not learned to express angry feelings, felt guilty because she felt the anger, and increasingly retreated from others, feeling more and more hopeless.

Some families can tolerate anger, but affection must be hidden. Children growing up in such a family are truly lovelorn, starved for affection, and terribly unskilled in expressing their own tender feelings. The inability to let others know one cares for them leads to all sorts of interpersonal problems.

Mary, a 23-year-old woman, sought help with her marriage. She indicated that her husband, John, seemed unable to express any affection. "He doesn't like to touch, hold, kiss—or anything. He never says, 'I love you.' On the rare occasions when we have sex, it's mechanical and seems to be distasteful to him." She described her husband's family as cold and distant. "John has never seen his parents kiss!" When asked if John expressed affection before they married, Mary explained that both of them had come from "very religious" families, and she had thought that John's lack of courting behavior reflected his religious principles and that he would change after they married.

In addition to the degree to which a family encourages the expression of feelings, the ability of family members to respond empathically distinguishes between families at different levels of health. Empathy is letting another know that you understand what he or she is feeling. It's a way of saying, "You seem angry, and I know what that's like," or "I've been there—and know how it is to be sad." Empathy is extremely important in human relationships because it leaves the other person feeling deeply understood and encourages further sharing and psychological intimacy. Families differ in this quality. Consider, for example, the dinner table conversation of two families with very different levels of empathy.

Family E

> *Father*: "Son, you're quiet and look down."
> *Mother*: "You really do . . ."
> *Son*: "Yeah—well, I don't feel very well . . ."
> *Daughter*: "Are you sick?"
> *Son*: "Ah . . . no . . . well, I didn't make the basketball team— Coach posted the list today . . ."
> *Father*: "That's really tough . . ."
> *Mother*: "Gosh—how disappointing. You've worked so hard to make the team. It really must hurt a lot . . ."
> *Son*: "It really does—I almost feel like crying . . ."
> *Daughter*: "I don't blame you—when I feel hurt I just want to go to bed and pull the covers over my head."
> *Father*: "Son—is there anything we can do—how can we help?"
> *Son*: "No—I'll just have to live through it—thanks, though."

Family F

> *Father*: "Son—you're quiet tonight. What's wrong?"
> *Son*: "Oh, nothing much . . ."
> *Daughter*: "Didn't they post the basketball squad today?"
> *Son*: "Yeah—I didn't make it . . ."
> *Mother*: "That really angers me—you're one of the better players—what's wrong with that coach?"
> *Father*: "Wait a minute—I'm really glad—now you'll have more time for your studies. Forget the basketball squad, son . . ."
> *Son*: "Yeah."
> *Daughter*: "Maybe you can play YMCA basketball."

In Family E, the family members responded to the son's disappointment and sadness with empathic statements. They acknowledge his feelings and let him know that they are "with him." As a result, there is greater likelihood that he will not feel alone in his disappointment. In Family F., there are responses (Mother is angry, and Father and Daughter rationalize), but no one responds to the son's sadness. He may, therefore, feel much more alone. Although these two families represent extremes, growing up in such families fosters very different views of what it is like to be human. In an empathic family, the developing child is encouraged to express feelings more openly because he or she learns that everyone has them and knows that they are important. In families low in empathy, there is often a failure to appreciate that all humans have feelings and that they need to be expressed.

A third factor involving feelings is the family's basic mood. Of course, there are variations in the prevailing mood of any family. For example, it may change from warm and humorous to serious and sad when the members hear of the death of a relative. The following day a disagreement between the parents may provoke a tense, hostile atmosphere. As that conflict is resolved, the family returns to its prevailing mood. Even with day-to-day variations, most families have a basic mood to which they return when problems or stresses are not present. Observations of a broad spectrum of families suggest that there are at least five basic family moods. These include:

1) *Warm.* The prevailing family mood is warm and caring; affection, humor, and optimism are present at high levels.

2) *Polite.* The prevailing mood is one of formality; some warmth and affection, as well as occasional hostility, are noted.

3) *Angry.* The prevailing mood is open anger; any evidence of affection or caring is lost in the constant blaming and attack.

4) *Depressed.* The prevailing mood is sad and despairing which may mask underlying anger. No humor or optimism can be detected.

5) *Hopeless.* The prevailing mood is cynical, pessimistic or, at worst, pervasively hopeless.

The degree to which a family encourages the open expression of feelings, the level of family empathy, and the family's basic mood are three important parts of the pattern of family communication. When considered along with the family communication style and the family problem-solving pattern, they offer valuable insights into the effectiveness of family communication and are directly related to the family's competence.

VI

Encouraging Autonomy

At this point in the history of our country the production of truly autonomous children remains one of the two important jobs of the family. A central premise of this book is that to the extent a family both produces autonomous children and stabilizes the parental personalities, the family can be considered competent or healthy. It has not always been that way, nor may it remain always so. Earlier in our history, for example, a family struggling to eke out an agricultural existence—at a time when most or all of the work had to be done by men and women rather than machines—needed to retain the young adult members of the family. If they married, they often stayed on the family farm so their productive energy was not lost. Under such circumstances, high levels of individual autonomy might not be valued greatly. The value of individual autonomy is dependent, therefore, to some degree on the circumstances in which the family exists. Even today, those families who, for example, operate a family business may require higher levels of interdependence and some sacrifice of individual autonomy. For many, if not most, families, however, the production of autonomous children is not clouded by mitigating circumstances and constitutes a central job of the family.

First, autonomy must be defined. Autonomy is based upon an individual's sense of separateness—the understanding that no matter how close one feels to others, how connected to family, spouse, or friends, how much like others one may be—there is a fundamental individuality present. Beyond experiencing one's self as separate from others, autonomy involves the capacity to function independently. An individual may sense his or her separateness, but rely so intensely on others that independent functioning is impossible. Autonomy involves both separateness and the ability to function on one's own. The autonomous person is able to separate his or her feelings and thoughts from those of others. "I feel . . .," or "I think . . ." is often used in conversation. Finally, the autonomous person is able to initiate activities rather than only responding to the behavior of others.

There are three aspects of the family that directly encourage the development of autonomy. These are the recognition and acceptance of individual differences, the capacity to deal with change and loss, and a reliance upon methods of communication that encourage individual expressiveness.

THE RECOGNITION AND ACCEPTANCE OF INDIVIDUAL DIFFERENCES

Families vary tremendously in the degree to which individual differences are recognized and accepted. At birth, for example, children in one family may differ strikingly in temperament. One child may be easy to raise, while another is difficult. Easy children often demonstrate a predominantly positive mood and seem to establish sleep-wake-eat rhythms quickly. If they are shown new objects, they tend to reach out for them. Difficult children do not have a predominantly positive mood, react intensely, fail to establish easily a sleep-wake-eat pattern, and retreat from new or strange objects. Between these two extremes, there are all sorts of different children. These differences are, in part, hereditary. Young parents often face having several children, each with a very different temperament. Some will be easier than others to relate to. Some will be seen to share a trait or two with a parent or grandparent, and this may be seen as either valuable or unfortunate. Accepting the individual child's unique physical and temperamental characteristics is crucial for the child's development, but may be difficult for the parents if there is something about the child that stirs up negative feelings. "This child is different" can be accepted by some parents and not by others. The foundation of the child's later autonomy is based, however, on clear messages of acceptance of his or her uniqueness. If the child is pressured by the parents, however subtly, to "be more like us or your brother or sister," or whatever is believed to be "good," the child may develop serious uncertainties about who he or she is or whether what he or she is can be "good." A short child in a family of tall individuals, a blonde in a dark family, a very active child in a family comprised of quiet and sedentary others, a shy youngster in an otherwise extroverted family—all of these differences can, if not accepted and cherished, come to be a source of uncertainty to the different one about his or her individual worth. Children growing up with a significant doubt about their value often are afraid to accept their individuality and do not venture out comfortably into the world of interpersonal relationships.

Henry and Edith James had four sons. Henry, a violinist in a major symphonic orchestra, was a quiet and studious man. Edith, an art historian, was more talkative; much of her life centered about her part-time job at the art museum. Their three older boys were studious, quiet, and self-reliant. Their youngest son, Joe, was physically the largest member of the family, devoted to athletics, and much more expressive than either his brothers or parents. He was also less self-reliant, but was skillful at getting others to do things for him. His differences from both his brothers and parents were a source of considerable concern to the family. His lack of interest in academic and cultural affairs was seen as both different and undesirable. His athletic skills were not responded to as strengths or assets. Without the necessary reinforcement of the value of his differences, Joe appeared increasingly reluctant to venture into new situations. His growth in the direction of increasing autonomy was slowed, and as the years passed he became more, rather than less, dependent on his family. Upon graduation from high school, Joe enrolled at the state university several hundred miles from home. He could not adapt, however, and became increasingly tense and depressed. He dropped out at midterm, returned home and, when his depression did not disappear, was referred to a psychiatrist by the family physician.

Joe's situation is an example of the relationship between a family's acceptance of individual physical and temperamental differences and the development of personal autonomy. Although many factors are involved in his inability to leave home successfully, his failure to cope with this developmental task and his subsequent depression were related to the many years during which his differences from other family members were not valued by the family. There was too much pressure (however subtle) to be like everyone else in the family. Since he was not like the others and his differences were not valued, he came to feel insecure and uncertain. His response was to cling to the familiar and not move out to begin a life of his own.

> Sally had always been different from the rest of her family. They were an outgoing, active group. Weekends centered about sailing, touch football, tennis, or water skiing. But Sally was less well coordinated, quieter, and more intellectual. She read extensively, wrote poems, visited museums and, in some ways, was a loner. Her mother said to the family researcher, "She's been different from the others since birth. She was later sitting, talking, and walking. Even as a little girl, she entertained herself—coloring books, playing games by herself. She seemed happy—it wasn't as if she was withdrawn—she just walked to a different drummer."
>
> Sally seemed to the research team to be a well-functioning teenager. She talked openly about her sense of difference from the rest of the family. "Actually, they're a rather rowdy bunch—always rushing off to do something. I sometimes think they all like to get hot, sweat, and take showers. Maybe that's it—I like to get into a hot tub with a book and stay and stay." Later, she reflected "being so different has made me kind of special. I'm the family intellectual—really, I'm not all that bright—it's just what I like to do."

In Sally's family, being different was not viewed negatively. Rather, her differences were seen as something special and valued. There was no pull on her to give up her individuality and be like everyone else in the family. As a consequence, Sally had a good foundation for feeling comfortable as she matured and moved towards greater autonomy. One would anticipate that she will have little difficulty leaving the family as she goes to college.

There are, in all likelihood, some biological and early developmental factors that give a child a head start in the direction of autonomy. Those children, for example, born with temperaments which include high levels of muscular activity and a reaching out towards novel objects may have a physical advantage over children with low levels of muscular activity and a retreat from novel objects. In a similar way, toddlers whose mothers encourage initial explorations away from mother may have a better start towards autonomy than those whose mothers encourage a tight clinging during this period of development.

ACCEPTING CHANGE AND LOSS

Things change; people mature and age; friends move away; loved ones die—there is movement in life, and some of it is sad and some joyous. Families must come to grips with the inevitabilities that life poses. This involves the family's ability to deal with time and its passage. In studying a broad range of families—from those doing very well to those in serious trouble—one is impressed with how differently families deal with the passage of time. For some, there is a fundamental acceptance. The flavor may occasionally be bittersweet, but there is an undercurrent of exploration for what may be best or unique about each period in life. Other families, however, do not accept the passage of time, but struggle to deny its reality or delay its impact. Parents in such families may search constantly for different ways to deny the inevitable changes. Quick to adopt each new youth fad, they seem to be searching for a way of dressing, dancing, or getting high that is, at the moment, "in." Often, there is a frantic quality to their search. Their message may be, "time is not passing; we are not getting older; nothing is changing."

Children growing up in families dealing so differently with the passage of time have different starts in the direction of autonomy. Those living in families who accept openly the passage of time and, as a consequence, the inevitability of loss, have a distinct advantage. The movement toward autonomy is aided by the acceptance of change. "As my parents get older, it is apparent to me that I am more and more on my own. Although I hate to think too much about it, someday they'll be gone and, in a way, I must be ready for that."

Children growing up in a family whose members deny the passage of time often feel little push toward separateness and autonomy. "It is as if things will forever be the same. I cannot imagine leaving—if I ever marry, we will live in this neighborhood and, if possible, on this street."

> The Harber family motto appeared to be "things will never change." There was simply a failure to acknowledge the passage of time. As the children graduated from high school, they went to the local university, lived at home, and found employment in the city. There was no consideration of leaving home, neighborhood, or city. When a friend or neighbor died, it was not discussed. Changes in the style of clothing were not acknowledged and, as a consequence, the family appeared to be living in an earlier era. The evidence that parents were aging was denied. The collusion appeared to involve each member of the family. It was a tight circle and there was little to suggest significant relationships outside the family.

Children growing up in such a family often do not feel self-sufficient. They may lack confidence in their abilities to venture out into the world. Initiative may be missing. They remain their parents' children far beyond the age of childhood.

COMMUNICATION THAT ENCOURAGES AUTONOMY

In the previous chapter, five aspects of family communication were discussed that contribute to a family's communication style. Four of these factors contribute directly to learning autonomy. Families who establish a climate of clear communication encourage their children to speak their thoughts and feelings with clarity. It is by being encouraged to say what is on one's mind that children (and adults) have the opportunity to learn the ways in which they are both similar to and different from others. This type of learning is crucial for the establishment of a sense of one's separateness. Without a sense of separateness, the individuals cannot move on to the level of autonomous functioning. Parents who frequently ask their children, "What do you think?" "What are your ideas?" or "How do you feel?" are actively establishing a climate in which each person is an individual with his or her own thoughts and feelings. Another way in which children learn is through direct observation of the parents communicating with each other. If each parent has the obvious right to his or her feelings and opinions and this separateness is accepted comfortably by each, the children have the opportunity to learn much about separateness and individuality. If, on the other hand, there is a strong push for sameness, or "we-ness," the children are apt to learn an entirely different type of relating. Contrast, for example, two families at dinner and consider the implications of the family conversations for the development of autonomy.

Family A

> *Father*: "The roast is good, Peg."
> *Mother*: "Thanks, I like it too. What do you think, John?"
> *Son*: "It's OK."
> *Mother*: "Something wrong with it?"
> *Son*: "No—I just like roast beef better than lamb."
> *Father*: "They really are different. I like them both, but I guess lamb like this is my favorite."
> *Son*: "Beef is juicier."
> *Mother*: "Yeah . . ."
> *Father*: "To each his own."
> *Mother*: "That's what makes the world go around—we're all different."
> *Son*: "Yeah."

Family B

> *Father*: "The roast is good, Marj."
> *Mother*: "Thanks. Do you like it Sally?"
> *Daughter*: "Well, it's *pretty* good."
> *Mother*: "What's wrong with it?"
> *Father*: "Sally likes it."
> *Mother*: "She said '*pretty* good.' "
> *Father*: "Probably not feeling well. You *do* like it, don't you Sally?"
> *Daughter*: "Yes."
> *Father*: "See—we all agree."
> *Mother*: "That's good."

In Family A, there was no prohibition against feeling different, but rather a tolerance for or encouragement of the clear expression of individual feelings and thoughts. The son in this family has an advantage in learning autonomy. He is growing up in a family who make it easier to be comfortable with differences by encouraging high levels of clarity in the communication of thoughts and feelings. The daughter in Family B has no such advantage. If that family's dinner table conversation is more-or-less typical for the family, Sally is not learning easily to express her individual feelings and thoughts with clarity. Rather, there is a push within the family for sameness. "We must all agree," if a strong enough mandate, can lead to lack of directness with others and even the denial to one's self of personal feelings and thoughts. This type of denial can directly influence one's movement towards autonomy. If individuals are consistently unclear or confused about what they are feeling or thinking, there may be a tendency to cling to the family and not move out into the world with all its uncertainties and ambiguities.

In a comparable way, families with a strong tendency to encourage family members to accept the responsibility for their feelings, thoughts, and behavior are setting the stage for the development of autonomy. Parents, for example, who gently insist that individuals not only speak clearly but accept the responsibility for the way they feel and think are aiding in the process by which individuals come to be comfortable with their differences from others.

Permeability, the acknowledgment of family members' messages, also contributes to a climate in which autonomy may flourish. Families who readily acknowledge each other's communications reaffirm the existence and importance of each other. To be with others who do not act as if one is present, who never respond to what one says, can be an anxiety-provoking experience of considerable intensity. To be a child locked into a family with low levels of permeability to each other can, over time, be devastating to one's sense of personhood. At the extreme, it may lead to profound doubts about one's very existence. At lesser intensities, it can lead to doubts about one's importance. In either circumstance, there is apt to be a retreat from separateness and self-sufficiency and a reluctance or inability to venture out into the world.

Invasiveness is the most deadly enemy of autonomy. To be told what one feels and thinks, if it occurs over and over again during the growing-up years, can lead to profound confusion about who one is. If, for whatever reasons, a parent wished to bind a child to him or her in a way that prevented the youngster from developing any sense of separateness, he or she would consistently and repetitively tell the child what the child is feeling and thinking. The difference between "Are you angry?" and "You are angry" is profound because the former seeks to clarify the individual reality of the other, whereas the latter seeks to dictate it. As autonomous adults, we can walk away from those who seek to dictate our reality. Dependent children cannot, and constant exposure to such adults may ultimately destroy the capacity for an individual reality. Fortunately, families with high levels of invasiveness are relatively rare in clinical practice. Most families—even those with considerable disturbance—do not consistently invade each other's inner reality. Only those severely troubled or chaotic families have been found to have high levels of invasiveness.

Children brought up in families who communicate unclearly, have low levels of responsibility, are impermeable, and invade frequently will have much more difficulty achieving autonomy. Children raised in families who speak clearly, encourage responsibility, demonstrate considerable permeability, and rarely invade will, on the average, achieve autonomy with fewer difficulties. There will, of course, be exceptions to the generalizations. Sometimes children who appear to be different from all others in the family may have a very different type of development. If one is born with both physical and temperamental characteristics which are different from others in the family, the differences may help or hinder the development of autonomy. In part, this is influenced by how the family responds to a child's differences, but another aspect is the issue of what an individual is different from. A child very different from other members of a family with low levels of clarity, responsibility, and permeability may have, by virtue of those differences, a greater opportunity to achieve a sense of separateness and subsequent autonomy than will brothers and sisters more like other family members. At times, then, it is decidedly advantageous to be the "odd" or different one in certain families.

> The Caller family was well-known at the mental health clinic. The father had been seen intermittently for alcoholism. Mrs. Caller was treated for severe and recurrent depression. Their twin daughters, age 25, had both been hospitalized for severe mental illness. Debbie, the quieter and more passive daughter, remained in the state hospital, and the family indicated that after three years they had little hope that she would ever rejoin the family. Her more active twin, Dorothy, lived at home and saw a therapist at the mental health clinic. She was unable or unwilling to work, and spent much of her time watching television with Mrs. Caller.
>
> Their youngest child, a son, Jim, left home for the Navy at age 17. On his infrequent visits home, he refused to attend a family therapy session with his parents and sister, Dorothy. A social worker had seen him individually, however, and reported that he had always felt different from his parents and twin sisters. "Even when I was little, I was different. I liked sports, being with people—I was always trying to get out the door to go play or watch a ballgame. Often, I had to sneak out. When I got older, though, they couldn't stop me." When asked to describe the family, he said, "The four of them are peas in a pod. They always think alike, but keep things inside. They're very quiet people—they can sit for hours without talking. I've always been different—more active and outgoing."

In this family, Jim's differences may have protected him from the high level of disturbance in the family and prompted him to leave the family shortly after graduation from high school.

In this chapter, we have seen the three basic ways in which the family encourages the development of autonomy. The first involves the acceptance of individual differences without any strong push for sameness. The second involves creating an environment that accepts the passage of time and the changes time brings to a family. The third focuses directly on those communication processes or ways of talking in the family that encourage children to accept and value their separateness and individuality.

VII

Intimacy

Intimacy is a term that describes a quality of relationship between two or more people. More precisely, it describes those moments when there has occurred a disclosure of deep and private feelings and thoughts. It implies a reciprocal process in which each person can share deeply from within and accept a similar disclosure from the other. Intimacy is usually a peak experience rather than a stable, constantly present state. Most people, for example, communicate at different levels at different times. The most superficial level is the commonplace. During this type of exchange, nothing of substance is communicated. "How are you today?" can be a cliché when there is no real interest, merely an acknowledgment of the presence of the other.

At a different level, there is exchange of information. Much of communication between individuals is designed to clarify the "what," "when," "how," and "why" of their activities together. At a more personal level, everyday feelings are expressed. Sadness, joy, disappointment, jealousy, fear, excitement, anger, and other feelings comprise a significant part of each person's life, and are shared in many relationships. The level of communication between individuals who are intimate, however, goes beyond the levels of the commonplace, the exchange of information, or expression of everyday feelings. It involves communicating feelings and thoughts that are usually regarded as deep and private. There is, for many, a sense of exposure or vulnerability associated with this level. It is as if there is something about the private feelings or thoughts that, upon sharing, might lead the other to think less, criticize, or reject. Although individuals differ greatly in the degree to which deeply personal communication involves a feeling of vulnerability, it is present to some degree for many persons.

These four different levels of communication can be seen in the following communication between a couple coming together at the end of the day:

Husband: "Hi. How've you been today?"
Wife: "Really want to know?"
Husband: "I guess I really didn't . . ."
Wife: "I didn't think so—you act as if your mind is elsewhere."
Husband: "It is—kind of . . ."
Wife: "What's been going on?"
Husband: "Well—might as well come right out with it. They didn't offer me the manager's job."
Wife: "Oh damn—who got it?"
Husband: "Jack Vernon."
Wife: "Why, he's so young—he's only been with the company a short time."
Husband: "I know—that's what makes it tough to accept.
Wife: "What a disappointment—you've worked so hard to prove yourself."
Husband: "I really am disappointed—hurt—kind of numb all over."
Wife: "Gee . . . I know it hurts . . ."
Husband: ". . . partly because I really was dreaming . . . kind of what I could do for you and the kids with the extra money . . . you've been so patient . . . I guess I thought that as manager I could prove to you how lucky you are to have me."
Wife: "Oh, honey, it's so sad that you feel that's something you have to prove. I had hoped that you knew—that deep inside you never doubted how I feel about you."
Husband: "I guess I should . . . but . . ."
Wife: "You—well, you know I've always seen myself as the little girl from the country—never dreamed when we met that I was attractive enough to interest you. All of my efforts—jogging and all that—it's all so I can look good to

you. I'm still just a little afraid that somewhere, someplace,
someone else will look better to you."
Husband: "We both carry some doubts . . . about . . . well, about
our value, I guess."
Wife: "It really is strange."

In this conversation, each of the four levels of communication can
be noted. The husband's opening, "How've you been today?" was
very commonplace. He was preoccupied with his own situation and
not really interested. The wife expressed her accurate observation,
and they moved on to exchanging information. She initiated this
change in level with her question, "What's been going on?" After
the sharing of information, he made the first move to the level of
everyday feelings with the phrase, "tough to accept." This couple,
with a relationship that allows the sharing of feelings, moved solidly
into this level of communication when the wife picked up on the
"tough to accept" phrase by responding with, "What a disappointment."

At this point in the conversation, the couple had done well. They
refused dreary banality; exchanged information clearly; and moved
on to important everyday feelings. This, in itself, is a considerable
accomplishment. They went further, however, and achieved some
intimate sharing. The husband revealed his private feelings and
fantasies regarding the importance of the promotion to him. In doing
so, he disclosed his fear of rejection unless he could do special things
for her. In response, the wife did not deny or ridicule these deep and
private feelings, but shared her own uncertainties about her own
value. At this point in their talking together, they had reached the
level of intimate communication. They might stay at this level for a
period of time—most often minutes rather than hours, days, or weeks
—and then move back to a less intimate exchange. However, repeated
experiences, like the one described, of receiving attention, understanding, and care, enable one to trust the goodwill of the other and
become more fully known—warts, wrinkles, fears, and inadequacies;
dreams, hopes, ambitions, and needs—to be able to discard the mask
which isolates many people even from their mates.

Why is this level of communication important? There are, perhaps, many answers to that question, but the most important factor

involves the sense of closeness and understanding that both individuals need and desire as an antidote to uncertainty and loneliness.
So much in life seems indecipherable or unknowable. Events that hurt
deeply can impinge upon us with breathtaking speed. There are many
occasions when a person feels alone and hurt or frightened—much
like a lost and bewildered child. We want someone close both at
such difficult times and also when great, joyful, and wonderful events
come to us. We are each separate and, at the same time, exquisitely
connected to others. A person's need to feel a bond with someone is
often at its highest level when strong feelings have been aroused. To
be in intimate communication at such times suggests an unusually
effective relationship.

HOW IS INTIMACY LEARNED?

Adults differ tremendously in their capacity for intimacy. The
fortunate ones seem unusually capable of intimate communication.
They are able to achieve the intimate level of communication not
only within the family, but also with a circle of close friends. At the
other extreme are those adults whose communication is entirely commonplace, who seem unable to be completely open with anyone.
However, most people can communicate both information and everyday feelings fairly easily, but seldom achieve more intimate levels.
"He's aloof—I never really know what he feels," or "She's a nice
person, but there's a certain wall around her, and she seems always
to be in control." If asked, many such individuals may deny the
importance of sharing deeper feelings or attempt to convert what
seems to be a personal liability to an asset. "It's better not to be
dependent on others" is a common response—as if the issue were
dependency rather than the capacity for intimacy.

Most of us enter adulthood with at least a beginning capacity for
intimacy, but it may need development. It's like a seed that may die
if it does not get proper nourishment.

What accounts for these wide variations in the young adult's
ability to communicate at the intimate level? Although there may be
a number of factors involved, most prominent is what we learned
about openness, closeness, and sharing feelings as we were growing

up in our families. Some families are good schools for learning intimacy, and others are not. If you are born into a family where deep feelings and private thoughts are shared openly, there is a strong likelihood that, as an adult, intimate communication will come easier for you. However, if you happen to grow up in a family where emotions and personal thoughts are hidden and intimacy is not possible, the odds are high that you enter adulthood at some disadvantage. The only way such persons have to learn about intimacy is from others—most often their spouses. If one's spouse is a good teacher, the learning deficit can be corrected. If, however, there is more than a learning deficit—severe underlying fears of intimacy— it may take more than a husband or wife with a good capacity for intimacy. Some individuals with fears of intimacy marry individuals with little capacity for intimacy, and such a relationship may suit both persons' needs. What is missed by one or both are those occasions when two persons can be very close.

What are the factors that make some families good teachers of intimacy? There are five that stand out: a strong, close parental relationship, family trust, individuality with closeness, warmth, and empathy.

The Parental Relationship

Parents are often unmindful of how much they serve as models for their children. They may rely on books or articles that deal with what the average child is thought to need at different ages or stages of development. Awareness of the importance of their roles as models for their children, if present, is often restricted to individual roles—that is, what a man, husband, father, or woman, wife, mother "ought" to be. However, children observe their parents interacting, relating, arguing, teasing, comforting—and these and other exchanges between the parents have a powerful influence on the developing children. Life in a family is more than a small group of individual personalities; it is also a constant process of interactions between members of the whole family, mother-father, parent-child, child-child. Families develop patterns of interacting, ways of communicating and relating that occur repeatedly. It is these patterns that comprise a significant part of life in the family.

The most influential relationship within a family is the parental marriage. Children make countless observations of their parents' relationship. Some have to do with a man and woman having a pleasurable interaction, while others involve the parents disagreeing, arguing, meeting crisis, or solving problems. Although intimate communication between parents often occurs when they are alone, it can occur when the whole family is together. A father, for example, may communicate at this level following the loss of a close friend. The open sharing of private feelings and thoughts comes, under some circumstances, to be seen as the normal way to do things. Parents, however, also suggest something of their capacity for intimate communication in indirect ways. The way they look at each other, touch, sit close, exchange barely perceptible nods—there are a host of ways that children learn a deep level of human communications, one that need not even be verbal.

There are many ways in which parents model or suggest intimate communication. Along with the direct sharing of intimate feelings and thoughts, the parents create an atmosphere of openness where this level of communicating and relating is an acceptable and desirable process. Whether the children are aware of the content of the parents' communication is probably not as important as their being conscious that it occurs.

Family Trust

Closely related to what children learn about intimate communication from their direct observation of the parents' relationship is the level of family trust. Families develop a basic attitude about the outside world. It is seen as a basically friendly place or as a fundamentally dangerous one. In interviewing or getting to know a number of families, one can deduce the basic family attitude. In our research, we described families as either affiliative or oppositional regarding human encounter. Some families respond to others as if the outcome of their meeting is apt to be good, interesting, warm, even caring. This basic affiliative attitude is a very powerful hypothesis because it is apt to precipitate a self-fulfilling outcome. If individuals or a family approach others with this basic attitude, it is likely to cause a friendly response from the others. This will not always happen, of course, for there are others who disregard affiliative overtures and maintain an oppositional stance. If, however, an individual or family has a basic attitude about human encounter that is oppositional in nature, it, too, will precipitate a reaction that fulfills the original oppositional attitude. If, for example, one meets a family at the beach and communicates distance, lack of interest, and suspiciousness, that family is apt to withdraw. Their withdrawal is then interpreted as evidence that confirms the family's initial impression that the world is a hostile and dangerous place.

This basic family attitude can be visualized as a line graph, rather than an either/or situation. At one end of the graph are strikingly affiliative families, and at the other end are strongly oppositional families. Most families can be located between these two extremes.

A family's attitude regarding human encounter is related to their basic assumptions regarding the nature of being human. Affiliative families are likely to think of humans as fundamentally good and to view destructive behavior as a response to difficult circumstances. Oppositional families are more apt to think of humans as essentially evil—sinful, aggressive, exploitative—and to feel that what passes for goodness represents the constraints offered by a society. Families at either end of the graph relate to others in ways that confirm their attitude—whether affiliative or oppositional—and their internal picture of man's nature—whether good or evil.

Children growing up in affiliative families have the opportunity to learn about trust. This experience encourages one to share more of one's self with others. A family that encourages this type of trust also offers the freedom to share more deeply private feelings and thoughts. The message both within the family and regarding the outside world seems to be, "Let the others know what you really feel and think. Do not be afraid—you will not often be hurt. On those rare occasions when your sharing leads to hurt, try to learn what went wrong."

Individuality With Closeness

One of the findings from the study of healthy families is that intimacy can occur only between persons who are separate, who have a clear sense of their individual identities—people who know what they feel and think as well as how they differ from others.

There are three possible combinations of separateness and closeness noted in different families. Healthy families demonstrate both high levels of individuality and high levels of interpersonal closeness. Certain dysfunctional families show high levels of individuality or separateness, but little in the way of closeness. Very disturbed families reveal little in the way of individuality or separateness and display a kind of sticky togetherness. This type of togetherness is not healthy closeness because each individual gives up too much of his or her individual identity in order to be a part of the family. At first glance, such families may appear close but, in reality, their personalities merge in a glob that wipes out the boundaries between the individuals.

To be a child in a family where individuality is encouraged in a climate of warmth and openness is to be prepared for adult intimacy. Parents who encourage their children to put their opinions, feelings, and ideas into words are helping those children learn how they resemble and how they differ from others. To be able to recognize and understand one's individuality in a family atmosphere that is accepting of those differences allows one to develop comfortably. This may lead to the capacity to value the variety and richness of others as individuals who are different. The ability to accept others as different promotes intimacy. However, to the extent that one is unable to accept that another is different and may feel differently about something, one will either not be able to hear where the other is or will struggle to convert the other to one's own attitude or viewpoint. An acceptance of one's own separateness paves the way for accepting the differences of others and opens the way to intimacy.

Family Warmth

Families vary tremendously in the amount of warmth encouraged between family members. Every family has problems, conflicts, and crises, but most families have a customary mood to which they return when not dealing with significant stress. For more fortunate families, the everyday climate is warm and caring.

It is important to understand that human warmth involves two messages. The first, and most obvious, is "I like you." The second, and less obvious, is "I want you to like me, too." My colleague, W. Robert Beavers, has emphasized that an important element of communicating warmth involves letting the other person know that he or she is needed.* It is the freedom to exchange vulnerabilities that makes warmth essential to intimacy. One needs both to care about the other and to be comfortable with one's need for the other in order to make intimacy possible. Persons who appear remote and uncaring about others may be more fearful about needing others than they are lacking in care for others.

It is, then, families who accept their need for each other as well as their affection and care who prepare their children for intimacy.

Empathy

Families differ in the extent to which the open expression of feelings is encouraged. Some families encourage the expression of all feelings, others of only some feelings, and a few families prohibit the direct expression of most feelings. In response to expressions of feelings, some families show a remarkable capacity for empathy. "I know what it is like to be sad, happy, angry, hurt, or whatever," involves both the ability to perceive sensitively what another is feeling and the capacity to let the other know that he or she is understood. It is a "being with" another person that implies no judgment about what the person is feeling.

It is doubtful that individuals are born with empathy. Fortunate infants with sensitive, responsive mothers may experience empathy very early. For example, it is striking that some mothers learn quickly the difference between the infant's "I'm crying because I'm hungry" and "I'm crying because I'm wet." Being cared for by such a mother may be the start of learning about empathy.

As children are growing, they are greatly influenced by the level of empathy of their family. When their families are understanding and expressive, the children gradually come to expect empathy and

---

* Beavers, W. R. *Psychotherapy and Growth: A Family Systems Perspective.* Brunner/Mazel, New York, 1977.

to feel empathic. This obvious lesson is of major value in diminishing the sense of vulnerability that is often involved in intimate communication. Such individuals do not learn to fear that sharing deeply held feelings and thoughts may lead to ridicule or rejection.

THE SEARCH FOR INTIMACY

Many individuals continue to grow in their capacities for intimacy throughout their entire lives. Except for those whose earlier experiences hurt too deeply, there is a continuing search. It is as if there is a sense that such is possible and highly desirable. A clinician often finds that one partner in a troubled marriage has a greater need for intimacy than the other. During the middle years in a marital relationship in which there has been little intimacy, one partner may begin to feel its absence. Frequently, the tragedy is compounded when the needful partner searches outside the relationship for intimacy. I suspect that more extramarital affairs begin for this reason than any other—the simple yearning to be close and to be understood.

> A 46-year-old engineer sought help because of marital problems. He reported that he had been happily married for 22 years. "In retrospect, Doctor, I didn't realize what I had been missing. We liked the same things, and I thought we had a good marriage. The kids were in the center of our lives and I was terribly busy with my career. Just when the children were practically grown and gone and my career was very successful, I began to feel a vague sense that there ought to be more to life. I tried talking to my wife about it—but she really didn't seem to understand. One night I worked late at the office and began talking to one of the secretaries . . . and, well . . . I've been able to tell her more about me than ever before to anyone. We meet often, and it has become a sexual thing too. Most of all, though, it's just talking—really talking."

This man had reached a stage in life where he was well respected and economically successful. It did not bring him, however, all that he needed, and he became aware that he and his wife did not communicate at an intimate level. His attempts to change this with his wife were half hearted, and another person was readily available.

He quickly turned away from his wife, but he felt guilty and confused.

This man's dilemma is not rare. Although his extramarital affair eventually included sexual expression, it was based on his need for intimacy. There were, of course, factors that help us understand why he so quickly turned away from his wife in his search. She was a very self-sufficient person who had adapted to a marriage in which there was little intimate communication. He, in turn, was fearful that she would scoff at his private thoughts. He felt less vulnerable with the other woman, and was stimulated by her obvious responsiveness.

Often, couples with many strengths in their relationships want to learn together the skills required for more intimate communication. Such learning and desire to grow can often produce significant change in fairly brief periods of time. It may be that intimacy is so important for most persons that it is never too late to learn.

VIII

Putting It All Together—
The Healthy Family

Some psychiatrists, psychologists, and other mental health professionals express doubt about the existence of truly healthy families. Often, they suggest that the world we live in is so uncertain, unpredictable, and unstable that stable family life is impossible. Although the world may be in unusually difficult shape currently, there are truly healthy families in it. One must seek them out because they do not come to the attention of clinicians. Most mental health professionals who spend their lives trying to help disturbed individuals and their families have intimate experience with only two families—the family they grew up in and their here-and-now family. To know only two families intimately, and then spend a professional lifetime dealing with disturbed families—or families under severe stress—simply does not provide detailed knowledge about healthy families.

If one wishes to study healthy families and announces such publicly, not all the families who volunteer will be healthy. Some will be families in trouble who are searching for answers. Nevertheless, there will be some healthy families who do volunteer, and these families are the focus of this chapter. Let me emphasize again that "healthy" means highly competent in raising autonomous children and maintaining the sanity of the parents. This definition of healthy families is a matter of values. Readers who disagree with the definition of what a family should accomplish are, of course, free to do so. However, the description of what goes on in healthy families is based upon the assumption that these are the primary functions of a family.

PARENTAL MARRIAGES

The title of the major publication describing the details of our research with families contained the phrase, "no single thread." That phrase reflected the finding that healthy family functioning was not the result of one strong factor. Rather, it seemed that 10 or 12 factors combined to account for these families' highly competent functioning. Although this point is important—having a healthy family is not like grasping the brass ring on the merry-go-round, but involves a number of factors—it is, nevertheless, difficult to minimize the importance of the parental marriage for setting the tone and tempo of life in the family. For example, researchers judging the quality of the parental marriage agree with other researchers' ratings of the level of competence of the whole family. The better the parents' relationship, the higher the likelihood that the family will be competent. The worse the parents' relationship, the higher the likelihood that the family as a whole will be in trouble.

Chapter III described "good" marriages. Each of the healthy families was characterized by this type of parental relationship. To recapitulate briefly, these couples shared power. Both parties were competent and had areas of special expertise. Because they had equal or nearly equal power, deep levels of intimacy were possible. Neither party felt that intimate communication was apt to lead to rejection or a competitive advantage to the other. They did not feel highly vulnerable. The emotional aspects of their relationship were rich and intense. They liked each other, were "good friends," and there was a strong bond. Despite the strength of their relationship, each was an individual —there was no fusion of personalities that blurred individual characteristics. They could tolerate and relish their differences. Each individual had several areas of interest or activity that were his or her "own thing." Although the other expressed interest and support, there was no resentment or competition.

The parents in healthy families had good sexual relations. For some couples, this was a central aspect of the relationship, and generally these couples had high levels of sexual activity. For others, however, sexual relations were less frequent and, although very satisfying to both, did not seem to be a central part of the relationship. They described their sexual intercourse as gratifying in different ways on different occasions. At times, it was a peak experience of intimacy, but other times it was more playful, adventurous, or purely physical sex. We did not ask for a detailed inventory of actual sexual practices, but most of these couples reported considerable freedom to experiment and did not feel bound by a rigid rule system to one technique or position.

The parents in healthy families were open with their feelings and showed high levels of empathy. There was little to suggest insensitivity to each other, but rather each was perceptive of the other's feelings. Conflicts and problems did occur, but were identified early, discussed thoroughly and, with few exceptions, settled quickly. As a consequence, there was no underlying, long-lasting tension resulting from unsolved problems.

If these marriages sound ideal to the reader, that is the way they looked to the research staff. It is important to emphasize that these marital characteristics were noted using a number of different ways of studying the marital relationship and were not simply what the couples said about their marriages. They felt fortunate, and often gave the credit to each other for what they realized was a wonderful relationship. "Anyone could have a great marriage with her (or him) —it's easy" was the most frequent explanation of the good fortune.

As might be suspected, there were no competing relationships. Children and grandparents were loved—but there were neither unusually close nor powerful alliances that competed with the marital relationship. None of the individuals had looked outside the marriage "for something better."

POWER

As suggested above, power in these families was securely in the parents' hands. But their style with the children was not heavy-handed. Rather, they provided a quality of easy leadership. They listened to the children's opinions and feelings with respect and often sought to solve problems and disagreements through clarifying the underlying issues, searching for a consensus, and suggesting compromise. Rarely did the parents appear authoritarian. The children, for their part, did not seem to resent the parents' power, but took it as a matter of course. It appears that the children were satisfied to know that their opinions were respectfully considered. When asked, "Who is the *real* boss of the family?" the common reply was: "Mother and Dad" or "Depends on the situation—sometimes Dad and sometimes Mother."

In this way, the differences between the roles of parent and child were clear. There was a "generation gap," but it was not an angry, conflicted one. There is not much for children to rebel against if they are treated as individuals and with respect.

The parents did face difficult decisions—the age at which girls could "car date" or when sons could have the famliy car at night. Parenting has many difficult moments, and these families were no exception to the rule. There was, however, no question as to who had the ultimate authority and responsibility. Sometimes, despite attempts at respectful problem-solving, the parents made unpopular decisions. On such occasions, the parents were together and united by their joint decisions.

FAMILY CLOSENESS

These families were closely knit. They shared a great deal with each other and felt strongly connected. At the same time, family members were individuals. Each had his or her opinions and feelings. There was no push to have everyone agree or to achieve a sameness or oneness that blurred individuality. This pattern of high levels of both individuality and closeness puts to rest the notion that to be really close to others, the individual must relinquish aspects of his or her individuality. Both closeness and individuality were found at high levels in these families and not in families seen as less competent or effective.

COMMUNICATION

These families communicated very well. They were clear with each other and there was little difficulty knowing what each other felt or thought. If a family member seemed unclear, others in the family requested clarification. The clarity of their communication, however, was not achieved by use of a stilted or excessively formal language. Rather, these families were very spontaneous, used a good deal of shorthand in talking with each other, interrupted each other frequently—and, despite this informal style, maintained high levels of clarity.

They were very permeable to each other; listening, they let each other know they had heard. The acknowledgment of individuals' communications took many forms—often with words, but frequently with a smile, nod, or wink. Although others might disagree, in these families the individual knew he or she had been heard and was understood. Individuals were expected to take responsibility for their own thoughts and feelings and neither to be obscure nor to blame others.

As a consequence of this pattern of family communication, the children spoke their minds clearly—"I feel this . . ." or "I think that . . ." were common expressions. Such individual feelings and thoughts were considered normal—and differences of opinion or feelings were taken for granted rather than seen as cause for argument. It was not a catastrophe to see something differently from other family members. It implied neither inferiority nor treason. It appears, therefore, that this pattern of family communication is a factor in the development of children with high levels of individuality and autonomy.

PROBLEMS IN THE FAMILY

Every family faces problems, and healthy families are no exception. There are several obvious aspects about the way problems were dealt with. First, these families identified problems early. There was no turning away from problems or denial of their reality. Rather, problems were very apt to be identified early and before they worsened. Second, there was very little blaming of individuals for the problem. The family accepted that mistakes are common and human, and rather than only venting anger at the person or persons involved, moved rapidly to a consideration of what to do about the problem. Third was the family's reliance on negotiation as an important approach to problem-solving. The open invitation to each person to express personal views, the search for a consensus, the working out of compromises—all of these were part of such families' basic approach to problem-solving.

As a consequence of the early identification of problems, the failure to blame the individuals involved excessively, and the use of problem-solving approaches that sought everyone's participation, there was no evidence of the lingering, beneath-the-surface problems that periodically erupt into warfare or crisis in other families.

FEELINGS

Healthy families are very expressive of feelings. The nature of the feelings does not make any difference. Whether angry, sad, loving, hurt, or fearful, the likelihood is high that they'll be shared. This level of expressiveness, and contributes to the attitude of openness observed in these families is not found in families of lesser competence.

When feelings are expressed, there is a good chance that someone else in the family will respond empathically. Empathic, "I know what it's like to feel that way," responses are important in several ways. First, by being non-judgmental they help the individual with the feelings to know that there is nothing abnormal about having the feelings. Second, they may lead the individual to feel less alone with the feelings. Third, empathic responses invite a more complete or further sharing. This invitational quality of empathic responses may lead to relationships of great closeness.

Most families have a basic mood. This is the general feeling tone within the family when there is no crisis. The basic mood of healthy families contains elements of warmth, humor, and concern for each other. Less healthy families have basic moods of a different quality. They may be mostly polite—or hostile, depressed, cynical, or hopeless. Living in a family where, more often than not, the mood is positive, the expression of feelings is encouraged, and empathic responses are frequent leads to an awareness that feelings are normal and to be shared—a type of openness with and about one's self that may characterized one's behavior in other situations. There is, perhaps, no other single individual quality that has such profound social consequences. Most people move towards, and want to be with, individuals who have this kind of openness.

DEALING WITH LOSS

Although the way a family deals with life's inevitable losses will be discussed in more detail in a later chapter, at this time it is important to point out that healthy families are more likely to be open with their feelings about losing someone or something important. There is no prohibition against being sad and sharing that sadness with others. Since the evidence is growing that losses that are not dealt with openly may play a role in a variety of illnesses, healthy families' tendency to deal openly with their losses may help to explain why they seem to have fewer illnesses.

THE FAMILY AND VALUES

Healthy families behave as if they have concluded that people are mostly good, rather than mostly evil. Their approach to human encounter is, for the most part, open and warm—or what has been called affiliative. This affiliative attitude about others is most often seen in the family's style when with strangers and may be contrasted with families who behave as if people are mostly evil. They tend to have an oppositional attitude towards others.

A related attitude about being human is the notion of mistake-making. Healthy families act as if people are prone to make mistakes—"to err is human." They tend, therefore, to see their own mistakes and those of others as simply part of being human. This leads to a disinclination to interpret the mistakes as intentional or even malicious. Although there are, of course, times when all persons do things that hurt others, many times such behavior is simply a mistake and there was no harmful intention. To have a basic understanding that to be human is to make mistakes helps in distinguishing between the impact and the intent of another's behavior.

Another related attitude about being human has to do with the complexity of human motivation. Healthy families react as if they understand that human motivation is complex. If, for example, the parents decide that a child's behavior warrants some type of punishment and, despite the punishment, the behavior persists, the parents are apt to reexamine their original thoughts about the behavior. "Maybe there is more to this than we originally understood" suggests that another's motivation can be complex. Under these circumstances, the parents are likely to try another approach in dealing with the child's behavior. Troubled families are more apt to behave as if human motivation is simple. If their initial attempts to deal with a child's behavior do not succeed, they are likely only to increase the intensity of their original response rather than considering alternate understandings of the behavior.

Finally, healthy families do not often rely on authoritarian rule systems. Individuals in such families respond to questionnaires designed to get at this part of life with strong non-authoritarian responses. If, in addition, one interviews family members in the attempt to understand how they support their basic values (which mostly are values having to do with the family and individual fulfillment), one finds that they rely on two support systems. "I've studied it, and the evidence points in this direction," and "Don't really know—that's just the way it feels to me" are two typical responses. One does not find statements like "The good book says it's so," or "That's what my daddy taught and it has to be right." One sees, therefore, that individuals in healthy families rely on rationality and feelings, but not authoritarian rule systems to support their basic value judgments.

INTIMACY AND AUTONOMY

If one wished to design a human system that encouraged both intimacy and individual autonomy, that system would be very much like the healthy families. The emphasis on clear roles, shared power, effective problem-solving, openness with feelings, acceptance of individual differences, and a basic attitude that teaches something about the good in people and, therefore, the value of trust is the kind of human network that would encourage both intimacy and autonomy.

At the same time, these families are very much involved with the world around them. They are not isolated, but are active participants. Despite the striking similarities in the way such families communicate and relate—that is, the underlying family processes—their styles may be very different.

FAMILY STYLES

Healthy families do not look like they were all pressed out of the same mold. It is only when studying how they relate and communicate that the similarities are discovered. What they're interested in, their general level of activity, the amount of excitement, their involvements in politics, religion, and other areas—all of these are quite different—and contribute to very different styles.

These differences can be appreciated by presenting brief composites of two very different healthy families.

The Searchers

Elsa and Martin Searcher and their 16- and 14-year-old sons, Paul and Merrick, appeared to be constantly looking for something. Elsa appeared in many ways to set the tone for the family. An active and dynamic woman with many interests, Elsa had great curiosity about the world. She knew who was lecturing where, what the symphony was playing, and which books were being discussed. She bought tickets for the family and encouraged participation. She seemed strong and almost dominant until one observed her with Martin. He was a quiet and successful accountant who seemed to enjoy much of his wife's involvement. "Although sometimes the pace gets too much—and then the boys and I will just say 'no more'—most of the time I like it. Elsa provides a kind of leadership that reaches out—she really feels we ought to sample it all. I tend to be more retiring and would miss a lot if it weren't for her."

The boys communicated great affection and respect for both parents. "They're very different—Dad's very solid—his head is on right—and he provides a kind of balance to Mother. She's terribly inquisitive and wants us all to do everything," Paul said, and did so with a smile. Merrick, at 14, put it differently, "I'm more into athletics and like rock. These aren't big interests of Mother's—but she's at every game I get into at school—she wants me to look at everything, but doesn't knock my own stuff."

Family discussions were lively and ranged from topic to topic. The family communication system was open—everyone had his or her say. There was obvious respect for each opinion, and evidence of affection and humor. Martin spoke less often than the other three, but when he did, they listened with obvious appreciation of his analytic skills.

In private interviews with Martin and Elsa, they each spoke highly of the other. Elsa described Martin as a source of stability that both allowed and complemented her "tendency to chase after every rainbow." Martin focused on Elsa's capacity to give of herself. "She's not afraid to expose herself—and us—to all sorts of situations—it's very easy for her to say, 'I don't know'—or 'I don't understand'—but then she insists on learning or, at least, trying it. Once in a while her feelings get hurt and, at such times, she . . . well, just wants to cuddle up and have my arms around her. I like that, too."

The Searchers were an active, "electric" kind of family. Their life as a family was fast-paced and frequently reached into the surrounding community. As a consequence, they were involved with other individuals and families with similar tendencies. There was no suggestion, however, that their searching activity reflected an inability to be together in quieter and more reflective ways. They had such times, but the style of the family was not constructed around those moments.

The Idlers

Harry and Jessica Idler and their three children, Becky, age 16, Monica, age 14, and Harold or "Buddy," age 9, were a pleasant family to study. They were an informal group and related with great spontaneity. Harry was a self-employed businessman who had achieved considerable success in an area that depended upon his skills in getting along with others. He was a casual, easygoing man who was very much interested in athletics. He played both tennis and golf and, although he most often played with male friends, he also played with Buddy. He was proud of Buddy's increasing skills in sports, and actively encouraged this involvement.

Jessica spent most of her time either at home or involved with the children's school and club activities. "I know it's not very fashionable, but I like being at home—the cooking, sewing—even the cleaning is satisfying. I have lunch or go shopping with friends about once a week—and that's fun—but what I like best is right here at home. Earlier in our marriage, I really tried golf and tennis—Harry is so into sports—but I'm not very coordinated and . . . well, . . . it wasn't that much fun for me—or Harry either."

When talking together, the Idlers appeared unhurried. They talked a lot about sports, family camping trips, the litter of pups Monica's dog had just delivered, or a television serial they watched together. The world of ideas or a strong involvement in the community did not appear to interest them. In their discussions, they listened to each other, respected the opinions of others, were open with feelings, showed high levels of empathy, tolerated differences, and were strongly affectionate.

In private interviews with both Harry and Jessica, the importance of sexuality was clear. Jessica stated that, with rare exception, she liked to make love every night. "It's so good—I like it all—the holding, the talking, and the actual physical sex. Harry is great in bed and I know he thinks it's wonderful." Harry, in his private interview, said that Jessica was wonderful in so many ways—"with the kids—here in the home—and . . . well . . . in bed she's fantastic. Occasionally, when I hear a friend make a comment that suggests that his wife doesn't like it—well, it seems inconceivable to live that way. From the start, Jessica and I have really been tuned to each other, and each year it gets better. We're more free with each other now than we were years ago."

The family was a smoothly integrated unit with no suggestion of ongoing or underlying conflict. Their considerable strengths as a healthy family, however, were, for the most part, directed inward. They did not have the level of outward involvement seen with the Searchers, but they were not isolated and did have good friends. The children's activities and a small circle of adult couples comprised the bulk of their relationships with the surrounding world.

Several of the experts who reviewed the Idlers' videotaped discussions, commented that many of this family's strengths were "in reserve"—that is, they were not in constant use dealing with the outside world.

The Searchers and Idlers seem, on the surface, to be very different. In many ways, of course, they are. Their striking similarities, however, are apparent when one focuses on how they relate and communicate rather than what their interests happen to be. Both the Searchers and the Idlers accomplish very well the two important tasks of the family. Elsa and Martin Searcher, and Harry and Jessica Idler are healthy individuals remarkably free from significant anxieties, depression, or other symptoms. When studied as individuals, they came across as different but stable and competent individuals. Paul and Merrick and Becky, Monica, and Buddy also are discovered to be doing very well. Each is in the process of becoming an autonomous adult. Although each has his or her own personality, they are, as a group, a bunch of healthy kids with evidence of age-appropriate emotional stability and independence, as well as social and interpersonal skills.

If we return to the original premise that stabilization or encouragement of growth in the parents' personalities and the production of autonomous children are the essential tasks of the family, we can understand that certain ways of relating and communicating are shared by families who do those two things well. The Searchers and the Idlers, however, help us to understand that we are not describing a monotonous sameness, but that the similar underlying family processes can be associated with remarkable differences in family style.

Tolstoy once said that healthy families are all alike. That appears to be so when one observes how a family relates and communicates, but it does not limit the striking differences in their approaches to life.

IX

The People in Healthy Families

What are the individuals in healthy families like? What characteristics do they share and how do they differ? How can we identify members of competent families? Now that we have some understanding of the factors associated with family health, let us turn our attention to individuals within these families.

In the descriptions of the adults and children that follow, it will be apparent that normal or healthy individuals are being described. In order, therefore, to place these descriptions in their current context, let me comment about the study of psychologically healthy people in general.

There is more scientific information available about individuals suffering from mental or emotional illness than there is about healthy individuals. There are several reasons for this. The professionals best equipped to study and understand health have been preoccupied with the many disturbed individuals and families who come to them for help. This follows a tradition in medicine in which illness and disease have often been studied first in the effort to find cures. Only later, and often as a part of understanding illness and disease, does the focus change to the study of normal functioning.

A second reason involves the amount of individual psychological disturbance present in our population. There have now been a number of studies of individuals picked at random or of all the individuals in a certain neighborhood or census tract. Although each study may have used slightly different criteria for evaluating the level of individual health, there is a strong similarity in their conclusions. Roughly, one-third of the people studied have emotional difficulties of enough intensity to interfere significantly with their day-to-day lives. Another third have evidence of emotional difficulties, with only modest interference in daily life. The remaining third seem to be reasonably free from significant emotional difficulty and could be thought of as normal.

A third factor derives naturally from the second and concerns the definition of normality. Even scientists use the term in different ways. One way, for example, suggests that normal means *average*. Using this definition in the large studies summarized above, one could conclude that the middle third of people with clear evidence of emotional difficulty but only modest interference in daily life should be considered normal. Another way of defining normal is as *optimal*—that is, the best possible level of adjustment or functioning. Using this definition, the third of the people without emotional difficulty would be considered normal. This definition is commonly used and is the one used in this book. However, this view raises questions such as "optimal for what?" It is apparent at once that this definition involves some value judgments. There is nothing wrong with this as long as one is clear. What would be normal or optimal in another culture or period of history might be very different from what is normal in here-and-now America. It is as if there is a preferred personality for a given place and time—preferred in the sense that it is most adaptive and productive for a given country's circumstances at a certain period of the country's development. A man, for example, who was a "loner"—didn't care to be around people, had few skills in getting along with others, and liked to work entirely on his own—might have the most adaptive personality in a pioneering country that depended on individuals establishing farms away from civilization and hacking out a life far from others. That man's personality would not be adaptive if he lived in an industrial city, worked on an assembly team, and lived in a crowded apartment neighborhood.

A fourth, and subtle reason that there have been few studies of normality is the feeling some people have that by studying and defining a normal person, one is saying something about the way all people "ought" to be. They fear that such a definition will lead to pressure for conformity—a conformity that may hinder the development of the unusual, unique, or eccentric individuals who are often unusually creative. Although this may be a risk, it appears that available research does not suggest that normal individuals are all alike, but rather that they share certain characteristics and differ in others much as the families described as healthy.

In addition to research focused on normal individuals, a number of prominent psychiatrists and psychologists—from Freud to Maslow and Menninger—have attempted to define the healthy person. Out of these sources, I would like to suggest that, in this country at this time, a healthy person would have all or most of the following characteristics:

1) *The ability to love, work, and play.*

The ability to love means, of course, more than falling in love. At its core, it means the ability to care for another as much as or more than one cares for one's self. It means the capacity both to give to others and to receive from others, thereby acknowledging one's own needs. It means the ability to share deeply of one's self with another and to know the other's inner self.

The ability to work means to be able, at least some of the time, to harness one's energy into an activity that one's culture designates as productive. Work includes not only selling, cutting out gall bladders, making soap, or trying law cases, but also painting pictures, taking care of children, or playing the flute in a small-town orchestra. Productivity, in this sense, does not imply a narrow, high-status definition, but speaks to the capacity to channel one's energy into activity that produces a service, product, or creation.

The ability to play means to be able to let go of one's work and to engage in activity that has, as its only or major goal, the sheer pleasure involved. For many, this means the capacity to return periodically to a form of activity more closely associated with childhood.

2) *Reasonable freedom from symptoms.*

Most people, including the healthy, do experience symptoms such as anxiety, tension, or depression. In healthy individuals, however, there are differences. The symptoms are usually of brief duration—hours, or a few days—and they are related obviously to stressful life events. One does not find enduring symptoms (weeks or months) that have no relationship to life stress. Generally, the symptoms experienced by healthy individuals are neither intense nor incapacitating. These factors—duration, intensity, and relationship to life stress—distinguish the symptoms of the healthy or normal person from those who have significant emotional problems.

3) *The capacity to deal with stress.*

Stress is an inevitable part of life. For some, life frequently involves exposure to harsh stress. The stress may be sudden, as with the death of a loved one; or enduring, as with poverty or prejudice. The capacity to endure and cope successfully with stress has limits. Each individual has a breaking point at which even unusual coping mechanisms or personal strengths can be overwhelmed by the sheer force or duration of stress. Individuals do, however, have vastly different capacities for coping with stress, and some individuals have specific vulnerabilities to certain forms of stress.

Within this general framework, healthy or normal persons have a well developed capacity to deal with stress. They may develop anxiety, tension, or other symptoms—but they deal as effectively with the stress as appears reasonably possible.

4) *The ability to master the stages of life.*

Closely related to the individual's capacity for dealing with stress is the ability to deal with the demands that different stages of life present. The concept that life can be seen as a series of age-related stages is, of course, an old one. In recent times, Erikson has proposed a timetable of overlapping periods of life, each of which involves a certain task or developmental problem that, if not successfully mastered, leads to a state of disturbance in the individual.* For some

---

* Erikson, Erik, H. Eight ages of man. In *Childhood and Society*. W. W. Norton and Co., New York, 1963.

years, the emphasis was on the stages of development occurring during childhood and adolescence, but the concept has been broadened to include the entire life span. The later years, for example, include the stage of generativity. During this period, the individual must face the problem of what he or she has been able, in broad terms, to generate. This could include, for example, ideas, products, or services to others. Failure to accomplish this developmental task often leads to a position of despair with a profound questioning of the meaning of one's life.

Normal or healthy persons successfully meet the developmental challenges of each stage of life. Although there is often pain associated with the life changes, the individual does master the challenge and, in the doing, demonstrates his or her capacity to change the tempo and direction of life. In a basic way, this characteristic of the healthy individual involves the ability to deal with change. One does not see a rigid clinging to an earlier period, the denial of change, and the minimization of life's inevitable cadence.

5) *The ablity to make the most of one's equipment.*

Persons are not born equal. Some come into life with major biologic advantages. Others, less fortunate, have physical equipment that is less than adequate. The first few years of life have profound importance because the infant is so helpless. Some infants receive a quality of care that remarkably nourishes their development. Others are exposed to an environment that is not at all conducive to healthy development. These physical and early developmental factors are not things that the individual has anything to say about—they are things that happen to the individual. They do, however, influence the quality of physical and emotional equipment one has for adult living. They limit the range of adaptation to adult life that may be possible. Thus, making the most of one's equipment is seen as a characteristic of healthy or normal individuals. "Making the most" may refer, for example, to dealing successfully with a physical handicap or low normal intelligence. The essence of this characteristic of health is the notion that there are limiting circumstances or deficits that must be taken into consideration in appraising individual competence.

With this background in mind, let us turn to a consideration of what the individuals in healthy families were like.

THE WIVES AND MOTHERS

The women in the healthy families we studied were in their mid to late thirties or early forties. With few exceptions, they were college graduates. As a group they came from intact, middle-class families, although a few had been raised by their mothers only. Although there were occasional exceptions, most described their families of origin in positive terms and had maintained close and caring relationships with parents and brothers and sisters. They described smooth development during adolescence, although some described themselves as having been shy or socially insecure. They did well in school, although there was considerable variation in the amount of intellectual and academic interest and achievement. As a group, they went to college more because it seemed the "thing to do" than as a result of a strong and clear career orientation.

Most of these women described their early years as free from periods of significant storm, unrest, or emotional problems that interfered with personal adjustment. There were exceptions: A few had periods of difficulty, and several had sought professional help.

Many of the wives and mothers had worked for a year or two prior to marriage, or until their first pregnancy.

With rare exception, these women pointed to their marriages as pivotal decisions in their lives. Although courtship or the early period of marriage was not always smooth, the evolution of an unusually successful marriage was seen as the aspect of life that had a profound impact on the quality of their existence.

> "As I look back, there is no question that marrying Drew was the most important decision I ever made. My friends from school who are now unhappy—or sour—well . . . they just didn't marry well or work it out or something. They are either divorced or unhappy—and, really, I don't see them much anymore—it's uncomfortable. I know it wasn't easy for Drew and me to work it out—the first couple of years we had a lot of adjusting to do—neither of us was really mature—and, it took me some time to really get into sex—you know—to really like and want it. He

really is wonderful—I feel terribly lucky—but, well . . . it does take two to make it go . . . If he weren't as kind and considerate —I need that. His sense of humor—well, we laugh a lot. The main thing, though, is that he let's me know where he is . . . he's good about sharing his feelings and doesn't shut me out. I really think I was kind of a normal gal back in college—but I think most of us were—and the thing that's made my life so good has been Drew and me."

Although the words were defferent and the intensity varied somewhat, this type of statement was made by each of these women.

Although a few of the women worked outside the home, as a group these women weren't wage earners. Their oldest child was 13 to 17 years old. The marriage, the children, and the home were the center of life. However, they had outside interests which varied from purely social to athletic or educational pursuits. These women had a great deal going on with others. With an adequate middle- or upper-middle-class economic base, there were no worries about the necessities. "We spend too much money—but do have a savings account, good insurance, a good company retirement program—and we do live within our income, but once in a while either John or I gets concerned about saving more, and then we do better for a month or so—but something comes along . . . well, it's living first for us—and saving is a poor second." It does appear that this level of relative affluence allowed these woman a considerable measure of social freedom. This was converted into a variety of involvements with others that permitted part of most days to be devoted to individual and away-from-home interests. What is important to emphasize is that these wives and mothers took advantage of the opportunity for involvement with others.

The women devoted a considerable part of their energies to mothering. Car pooling, club activities, den-mothering, and the rest were a part of it. It did not appear, however, that these activities were either disliked or frantic, but rather a fairly easy and accepted part of the mother's role. The children were seen as individuals, with valued individual differences. When asked to describe briefly their children, the following was a typical response:

"John is pretty much a typical 15-year-old, I guess. He's serious—maybe a bit too much—makes A's and is into science. He's a good basketball player—hasn't started really dating yet, plays his records too loud—well, what else? Let's see—he's really considerate—and usually nice to Kim and Les. He really admires his dad and has always talked to us a lot. Recently, though, he's perhaps been more to himself . . . I think, well, he's growing up and needs maybe to be and feel more private.

Kim is very different. She bubbles a lot—outgoing and has friends everywhere. She just started her periods—and, well, for a year or so has had some growth of her breasts—she's very proud—having periods and all that—and talks about it. She's more loving and affectionate—likes to touch you. She isn't nearly as disciplined as John—just as bright, I think, but well, things like grades aren't that important to her—she makes B's mostly.

Les is only eight and, at times, I think I baby him too much. He's a tough little guy, though. His whole life right now is his soccer team and he's very intense about it. He's not as well coordinated as the other two, but makes up for it with his intensity. He goes to school and doesn't have any problems with it—but I get the feeling that recess is the high point of his day. I almost lost him, you know, when I was four months pregnant—it was touch and go there—and, golly, maybe some of his specialness has to do with that, or maybe it's just because he's our last."

In private interviews, these women seemed open. They discussed their lives, hopes, and feelings with a refreshing candor. None had significant symptoms. Anxiety or tension of a mild degree was briefly experienced on rare occasions and always related to a real life stress. There were no persistent fears or phobias. Some experienced a mild "down" period prior to each menstrual period, but this was the exception rather than the rule. Most enjoyed social drinking, but did not use tobacco, and had no experience with sedatives or tranquilizers. As a group, they were able to discuss feelings openly. In discussing the death of a person close to them, it was apparent that each was able to re-experience some of the sadness.

Physically, these women were in good shape. They were attractive and well-groomed. None was obese. Their medical histories were characterized by the absence of life-threatening illness and minimal disability from their infrequent minor illnesses. For most, their only hospitalizations were obstetric in nature. As a group, they took no routine medicines except vitamins.

Julie Haller, at 37, a slim, dark brunette, had a style of relating that was open; she maintained eye contact and smiled often. She seemed poised and, at the same time, informal with the interviewer. She married Hal after her first year of college, and the following year, Karen was born. Three years later, their son, Howard, was born. At the time of the interview, Julie had gone back to college. She was taking nine hours and was pleased to be making A's. Her description of her life revealed the central importance of her relationship to Hal. She described him as a strong, ambitious, and hardworking man who "has more energy than anyone I know." She felt their relationship was unusually close, "We can talk about anything—and do." They made love three or four times most weeks and "more on trips." She experienced orgasm "almost always," and said that the sexual aspect of marriage was very important to both of them. Julie seemed, in particular, to value the confidence Hal showed in her judgment. "He really listens and encourages me to make my own decisions. Going back to college, for example, has changed our family life somewhat, but he encouraged me to make the decision. I think he's really pleased that I'm doing it—but it really is something I'm doing for myself."

Julie was remarkably free from symptoms. Occasionally she experienced mild premenstrual tension, but other symptoms were rare and related to stress. "Hal was offered a big job in Chicago, and we really talked it over. It was much more money and tempting. During those several weeks, I was a little tense—had difficulty going to sleep. Usually, though, I'm not the nervous type." She enjoyed a drink or two before dinner, did not smoke, and took no regular medication.

"Life has been great to me. The only real blow was losing Dad when I was 16. Hal and I really have a great thing going and both Karen and Howie are great kids—I have good friends, enjoy my courses—most every day is fun—at least some part of it . . . I'm not all that religious—though we go to church most Sundays—but God or someone must look after me. It really is a very good life and I'm a very fortunate person."

THE HUSBANDS AND FATHERS

Most of the men in this group were in their forties. As far as work was concerned, they were about equally divided between small businesses, the professions, and employees of large corporations. With few exceptions, they had positions of considerable responsibility and significant autonomy. Only a few worked in situations where they were closely supervised. The men worked long and hard and enjoyed it. In discussing their jobs, many focused on the satisfactions obtained from working with people. In particular, the men commented on the satisfactions involved in helping younger people achieve success.

As a group, the men came from middle- or lower-middle-class backgrounds. Often they were the first person in their families to have gone to college. Many were from small towns and had left to go to college or into the service. Most looked back on their families of origin with fondness and felt they had been raised in strong families. "We didn't have much—Dad was a mailman—but we were together a lot—had fun—and there were no serious problems." A few came from families with considerable problems—an alcoholic parent, serious illness, poverty, or parental divorce.

Without exception, these men were very invested emotionally in their families. Although working long hours, they found the energy to be involved with their wives and children. Family activities were important to them. Most such activities were "active"—athletics, camping, hiking, and this may, in part, have reflected the physicalness and activity patterns of the men.

These men felt extremely fortunate to have married their wives. It was clearly apparent that their marriages were at the center of their lives. They described relationships in which intimate communication was possible. "I've never been able to talk as freely with anyone as with Anne. I can't think of anything I could not discuss with her—that kind of freedom has a remarkable influence in my life—it is as if you don't have to be alone with any problem—unless, of course, you want to be. The most important decision I ever made was to ask her to marry me. She really is a unique person—loving, warm, open—and very bright—her mathematical ability is far superior to my own—and it's a pleasure to watch her mind work."

The men all felt that the sexual aspects of their marriages were excellent. For some, this part of the relationship seemed more important—at least both in terms of frequency of intercourse and the way the men described the relationship. "Jill and I have always loved to make love and we do so often. It's—well, the old cliché—lady in the parlor, tiger in the bedroom—and that's Jill. I'm very lucky that it's that way—because in some sense, I need it. It's not just the screwing—it's the being next to each other, the touching, the talk— the intense sense of being wanted."

As a group, these men were free of symptoms of emotional disturbance. Although they experienced tension occasionally, it was related to life events or important decisions. There was no indication of anxiety, tension, or depression unrelated to life events. The men, for the most part, were well-disciplined, orderly in thought and action, revealed evidence of considerable conscience, and had good capacities to be in touch with and share their feelings.

Most of the men enjoyed an occasional drink; a few smoked; none was taking any medicine regularly. None had ever had a tranquillizer. Most were active physically, and some worked out on a regular schedule. A few were several pounds overweight, but there was no real obesity. As a group, they had experienced no life-threatening illnesses.

Hal Haller was a large, friendly man. Slightly balding, he had the appearance of an athlete who had begun to age. He worked as the regional manager for an insurance company and had 30 agents who reported to him. His boss was located several thousand miles away, and he liked that. "I get along very well with him and, for that matter, all of upper management—but I like being mostly my own boss. I like my work—most of all working with the men—helping them, teaching them, watching them succeed—and, I guess, feeling that I've played some role in their success. The company offered me the opportunity to take the entire Midwest, but it would have involved moving to Chicago. We turned it down—and Julie and I talked a lot about what we wanted out of life. You see, if I had done a good job there, I probably would have been in line for head of sales, and that would have meant eventually moving East. We just decided we were too damn happy—had what we wanted here—and that we wouldn't move."

Hal discussed his marriage in glowing terms. "Julie is just one hell of a woman. She's bright, beautiful—and, most of all, very loving. Oh, we sometimes argue—but it really is rare. Almost all of the time things are good with us. At the center of it, maybe, is our sexual relationship—we really do enjoy each other. She's wonderful in bed—active, responsive—and, at times, takes over—I tell you, it's really wonderful. . . . Julie is very well—independent—and I like that. She is very self-sufficient—has no trouble making up her own mind—and yet, if we see things differently, she's easy to work out a compromise with. Most of all, we're friends—we really just enjoy each other's company—best friends, really."

Hal discussed his children at some length, and it was obvious that he and Julie saw the children in similar ways. He was teaching them both to play tennis, and he and Howie played golf together on Saturday mornings and had season tickets for the local university's basketball season. As a family, the four of them enjoyed camping, water skiing, and other outside activities.

"We also have two or three couples we're close to—Julie and I go to dinner with them—and, occasionally, the theater. The couples are much like us—about the same income level and all. We do have some differences about politics—Jack and Eve both teach at the university and are more inclined to take a liberal stance—but the discussions are fun and friendly."

THE CHILDREN

The children in these families ranged from age five to 17. As a group, they were remarkably healthy. They related well to the interviewer and discussed experiences, relationships, and feelings with openness.

They were all doing well in school although, for a small number, there was some parental concern that they weren't doing well enough. "Joe is very bright—he tests out very well—but makes mostly B's in school. He really doesn't work at it and we have been tempted to push him—study hours and that kind of thing—but we haven't. Just decided that if he's going to catch fire academically he'll do it—and we can't do it for him."

The children described positively their social relationships with other children. All were very involved with others and in many activities. Most were active in organized athletics—soccer, for the younger children, and tennis, for the older ones, were common.

The older children had begun to date, and a few had steady boy or girl friends. None used drugs or alcohol—they considered themselves "straight," and some talked of "not needing drugs to feel good or have a good time."

The children, without exception, admired their parents and felt they had good relationships with them. Mothers were more often seen as "easier to talk to," and the older children were the only ones to acknowledge having some secret thoughts they did not share with their parents. When asked who was the boss in the family, the most common response was, "Mom and Dad," and the children seemed to accept that as perfectly all right.

In these families, older children were more disciplined, controlled, and studious. Younger children were less so, and were somewhat more open with their feelings. "Karen is—well, kind of serious—studious—asks a lot of herself. Howie is very different—more spontaneous and less disciplined. He's more open with his feelings—a very loving little boy." The interesting observation was that these characteristics were related to the order of birth and not the sex of the child. In troubled families, these differences were noted, but more often boys were disciplined and studious and girls more emotional and expressive—regardless of their order of birth.

The children did not report symptoms that suggested emotional problems. There were not any fears except the occasional younger child who did not like dark rooms. There was no significant rebellious behavior and no evidence of diffuse anxiety. Almost all of the children said they occasionally felt anxious—"before a test" or "before a soccer game."

Karen and Howie Haller were engaging youngsters to interview. Karen, at 16, looked much like her dark and attractive mother. Physically well-developed, she appeared older than 16, and her considerable poise added to this impression. She was a junior in high school and very active in extracurricular activities. A "straight A" student, she was considering a prelaw major when she entered college. Karen dated several boys, had never gone steady, and was a virgin. She did not smoke and never tried drugs. Her only drinking had involved a glass of wine with her parents. She felt close to both parents, but talked more easily with her mother. She saw her father as a very bright and caring man and thought her parents had an "ideal relationship."

In describing herself, she acknowledged being "more serious" than some of her friends. School and making A's, though, were "easy." She denied anxiety, depression, disturbing thoughts, or unusual fears. She enjoyed reading, tennis, and family camping trips.

Howie, at 13, was blonde, an inch taller than Karen, and had a gangling look. He was intensely interested in sports, and had recently made the junior high basketball team. He wanted to be a professional athlete—"tennis or basketball," and described his happiest times as when he was involved in sports. School was "OK," but "nothing special"—he knew his parents would prefer better grades. "I make B's—but Karen's such a brain—she sets a bad example," he said with a smile.

There was an open, warm, and infectious quality to this tall and engaging 13-year-old. He liked people and seemed to anticipate that others would like him. He was not interested in girls —"they bore me'——but guessed he would come to that—"most guys do." He felt anxious only before athletics and had no fears or "down" periods. He did not believe in drugs, tobacco, or alcohol—"they would interfere with your ability to play sports."

The individuals in these families were healthy or normal individuals. They appeared that way to the psychiatrists and psychologists who interviewed them, and also in the results of the psychological tests they took. Although life is uncertain at best, these men, women, and children appear to have the stability and strengths to face the future with some confidence in their capacity to adapt to change. Their most important, supportive networks, their families, provide them with additional strength. They are, indeed, fortunate.

X

Faltering Families

Under circumstances which can be considered most favorable for the development of healthy family functioning, including relative economic security and lack of racial or religious discrimination, many families fail to reach high levels of competence. Actually, there are no facts which tell us what proportion of all families achieve the level of competence described in Chapter VIII. What is known is that there are many families which fail to one degree or another to accomplish the two basic tasks of the family. Some fail miserably; others just miss. This latter group can be called faltering families—they have competence but there is considerable pain within the family.

The specific problem with these families is that the relationship of the parents does not meet the emotional needs of either spouse. As a result, there is dissatisfaction, sadness, anger, blaming, and their consequences in these marriages. In areas that are not related directly to the emotional relationship between the parents, these families do well. The children are healthy and the family generally solves outside problems efficiently. In effect, such families do well one of the two tasks of the family—that is, raising children who appear to be moving toward independence and autonomy without evidence of emotional disturbance. They do less well in the task of nurturing the emotional stability of the parents. The parents are not disabled by emotional symptoms, but their unhappiness makes the future appear uncertain.

The most common pattern is that of the unhappy wife and detached husband. The wife feels deprived, her needs for closeness and intimacy unmet. She is apt to have a sour outlook, to feel she is missing an important part of life, and to eat too much and have a weight problem. She may see her physician often and be considered depressed. Chemicals in the form of mild tranquilizers or antidepressive agents may be prescribed. Her earlier dreams of the good life have not become reality. For all of this, she blames her husband. She points out that he is detached, remote, and keeps all his feelings, except, perhaps, angry ones, hidden. He is said to live within himself. "I never know what he's feeling and he's not interested in what I'm feeling," is a common complaint. "I'm starved for affection—not sex, but affection. I want to know that I am loved; I want to touch and be touched."

The husband describes things from a different perspective. He sees his wife as nervous, a whiner, obese, demanding, and difficult to love, "She doesn't take care of herself, usually looks like hell—but wants to be treated like a princess. She needs so much that no one could make her happy."

When interviewed, the husbands do seem to be remote. They are not openly expressive of feelings, and seem to be very private persons. Although as successful economically as the husbands in healthy families, they do not talk about their work as bringing satisfaction from people. Relationships at work are discussed from the viewpoint of the problems they pose. Satisfaction is to be found in sales performance, law cases won, or the quality of service delivered—not from working with people. Although their families are important to them, they seem to have little except money to give their wives and children. Their hobbies are apt to be solitary—woodwork, sailing small boats, and other activities to be done alone.

There is truth in the way the husbands and wives see each other. The men are remote and uncomfortable with deeper feelings. The women are sour, do whine, and are difficult to like. What is important is that each can see only the other's contributions to the distressed relationship and is blind to his or her own deficits. Both must share the responsibility for their failure and, if the relationship is to improve, must stop "making a case" about the other and come to understand their personal contribution to what is an impasse in their relationship. What happens too often is that the problem is assigned only to one of the two—and, more often than not, the wife may become a patient.

The failure of the couple to achieve the intimate level of communication is the central flaw in these families. It mars what could be a much more competent family. How, then, does the family look in other regards?

The parents tend to evolve an unequal relationship. The underlying struggle for emotional gratification casts an oppositional tone to the relationship. Each sees the other as hostile. "If it weren't for you . . ." can lead each to the search for advantage over the other. There can be, therefore, a subtle competitive edge to the relationship or the establishment of a pattern of dominance and submission. Both husband and wife may seek gratification from someone else. Most commonly, it is a family member—the development of a charged and "special" mother-son or father-daughter relationship. Such coalitions are compensatory in the sense that they evolve in an effort to make up for the emotional intimacy lacking in the parents' relationship. In such parent-child relationships, the parent invites or pushes for a level of intimate communication that is not appropriate for the developing child. Particularly destructive to the child are the coalitions in which the parent shares his or her dissatisfaction with the spouse, often describing in detail all of his or her "failings." This may lead to a serious split in the family and to the child's seeing one parent as "good" and the other as "bad."

Coalitions can evolve outside the family also. Perhaps the most common of these is either the husband or wife evolving a special relationship with one of his or her parents. "In-law problems" may be of many different types, but the special coalition in which there is greater intimacy than in the marital relationships is common. Outside coalitions, of course, can develop with friends and lovers. These, more often than not, develop as attempts to find a relationship in which intimacy can occur. Extramarital affairs may be started in the search for intimate communication more than out of sexual frustration.

The parents' sexual relationship is rarely good in these families.

The underlying emotional conflict may spread to interfere with sexuality or, as one wife said, "the screwing is good, but we don't talk." What is missing is the attitude of deep satisfaction so prominent in the reports of both husbands and wives in healthy families.

The family suffers from the lost opportunity to be close. There is no problem with separateness or individuality. The persons in faltering families are individuals; there is no pull for a fusion that would obliterate the individual's sense of his or her uniqueness. Closeness, however, is not achieved as it is in healthy families. The parents do not present a model of closeness that becomes a part of the total family atmosphere.

Faltering families communicate thoughts and ideas clearly. There is no mistaking what people mean. The individuals frequently acknowledge each others' messages—that is, they are permeable. These families insist on family members' taking responsibility for individual thoughts and behavior. In sum, these aspects of the family communication patterns were similar to those found in healthy families.

For the most part, problem-solving was effective. If the family has evolved a pattern of one-parent dominance, this parent is apt to do a disproportionate share of the problem-solving. As a consequence, negotiation as the primary approach to problems is less commonly seen.

In regard, however, to feelings, these families reflect generally some of the underlying conflict in the parental relationship. Faltering families are not as open with feelings as healthy families. There is avoidance or masking of feelings as if the family must step gingerly around some feelings in order to avoid the possibility that the conflict between the parents might surface openly. As a consequence, faltering families do not present the general picture of a group in which everything is out in the open. Their basic mood is often more polite than warm, joyful, and humorous. Empathy is present, but only occasionally. The tone and cadence of the parents' failure to achieve a relationship emotionally gratifying to both cast a constant quality of inhibition on the whole family. It is as if that conflict might explode and the family members avoid lighting the fuse by giving up the kind of spontaneous openness with feelings found in healthy families.

The way in which faltering families fail is that they do not produce an environment conducive to intimacy. The failure results in a family that does not support the personality stabilization or growth of the parents' personalities. Although we did not find mentally ill parents, neither did we find the high levels of individual psychological health seen in the parents in healthy families. The mothers appear to be bearing the brunt of the pain. They are unhappy, sometimes moderately depressed, often angry, and nearly always had some physical symptoms. Although their descriptions of their husbands' difficulty sharing feelings and consequent emotional remoteness seemed accurate, they do not perceive their own roles in the marital distress. Their blaming of their husbands is total.

At this point, what happened to these women is not known.* Many professionals might speculate that their futures are uncertain, that significant depression awaits them. Others, however, would emphasize that, as a group, they have many strengths and have ways to deal with their disappointments and frustrations that will help avoid depression. Perhaps they will return to school or take courses, increase their involvement in community activities, or find other pursuits that will provide emotional satisfaction lacking in the marriage. They do, however, appear vulnerable.

The husbands also seem to be missing something. Emotionally isolated, keeping their feelings inside, they forge through life alone, getting satisfaction from material objectives and career performance. Although without the symptoms of their wives—unhappiness, physical complaints, a sour, angry attitude—they are without intimacy. Intimate communication is not apparent in any of their relationships. It is tempting to speculate that their business and professional successes are rewarding enough to prevent the development of symptoms, a type of satisfaction their wives do not obtain. One may speculate that they, too, carry an increased vulnerability to depression at a later stage of life when most of their career goals have been accomplished.

It is important, however, to emphasize that these men and women

---

* Follow-up study of these families five to seven years later is underway at the time of this writing.

believe in the importance of their families. Most of the family emphasis is on the children—their growth, development, and activities. These parents appear to be genuinely concerned and involved with their children. As a consequence, the children appear to be flourishing. As a group, they cannot be distinguished from the children in the healthy families. Interviews and testing both reveal evidence of healthy growth and functioning. The children are doing well in school, have good relationships with others, and exhibit a striking freedom from symptoms such as fears, withdrawal or anti-social behavior. Although they are not as open with their feelings as the children from healthy families, they do appear to be making excellent progress in the development of autonomy.

It is encouraging, therefore, to conclude that healthy children can emerge from less-than-healthy families. It does not require the level of family competence seen in the healthy families to insure the development of children who appear free from emotional problems. Nevertheless, one may speculate that, as adults, these children who have not had the opportunity to learn intimacy—to observe adults who express feelings openly—will have limited ability to enter adult relationships in which intimate communication occurs fully.

Alice and Mike Fortran and their children, Amy, age 16, Harold, age 14, and Susan, age 11, seemed to be an ideal faimly. Mike was a successful attorney with an excellent reputation in the city. Their home was fashionable and reflected Mike's economic accomplishments clearly. Their neighbors saw them as a solid, if not ideal, family. They were active in the neighborhood and school functions, and attended all the events in which their children participated.

Mike was known in the neighborhood as a quiet man. He seemed reserved and was often noted to be working alone in the yard. He played tennis, but only singles. Occasionally, he played with Harold, but more often, no member of the family was involved. Mike exercised regularly and, in particular, jogged alone each morning. He was one of the younger partners in an established law firm, and was often involved in actual court work. He was intensely competitive, and it was apparent that he enjoyed the head-to-head battles with opposing lawyers.

Mike had no really close friends. Two or three attorneys in the firm were friends, but the relationships did not involve sharing intimate feelings or thoughts. At work, Mike was known as a bright, hard-working perfectionist who had a "steel trap" mind. He did not negotiate easily, finding it difficult to compromise, nor did he participate in the firm's public relations by entertaining or participating in civic work.

Mike described himself as "somewhat of a loner." He was not demonstrative, nor could he tell others that he cared for them. "I live mostly within myself—maybe a secretive kind of person or even a little inhibited." Mike could, however, talk with the interviewer about his feelings for his children. He said that he loved them very much and was proud of their accomplishments. "I think they know I love them—but it is hard for me to show it openly. I don't hug or kiss very easily."

In discussing his marriage, Mike emphasized Alice's skills as a mother. "She's really great with the kids—just seems to know what's best for them." When asked specifically about his and Alice's relationship, he said that he thought it was a good marriage—"better than most." He felt that during the past few years Alice had become "nervous," and he wondered about "an early menopause." "She's sick a lot and, of course, overweight. She won't exercise, and I disapprove of the tranquilizer she takes from time to time—even though it's a mild one." Mike did know that Alice felt he was "hard to get close to," and felt there was truth in that impression. "Most of the time, however, when she wants to talk, it's late at night—I'm tired and have to be in court early. Often, too, what she wants to talk about are unhappy topics—she's not very much fun to listen to." Their sexual relationship was "fair"—"after a few drinks she may warm up—but usually it seems like a perfunctory performance on her part. We don't make love very often anymore—maybe once or twice a month."

Alice was known in the neighborhood as a much more friendly and outgoing person. She knew all the neighbors and had coffee or shopped with several of them frequently. She was 30 pounds overweight and expressed concern about her obesity but "not enough, I guess, to really do anything about it."

Alice saw her gynecologist most months. "I have trouble with my periods and am very nervous. Then—out of the blue—I'll have a down week and feel like going to bed and crying. Doctor Morton gives me mild tranquilizers—I don't take them all the time, but just when I feel bad. They seem to help—to take the edge off."

Alice maintained a cheerful composure during the interview

until the subject turned to her marriage. At this point, she became tearful and later angry. "Mike is such a good man—he doesn't run around, he makes a good living, and I know he loves his family. I talk a lot to my mother, and she says I ought to realize how lucky I am—and, yet, it's not much of a personal relationship. Mike is so reserved. He hardly tells me he loves me, and I never really know what's on his mind. There's a wall around him. I need so much more—talking and sharing, touching—and, well, just a lot I don't get. I find myself wondering what it would be like with another man. I think I'm starved for affection and closeness, and often I get angry at him. It doesn't do any good, though . . . he always wants to know something specific that he's done. I'm sure my nerves and overeating have something to do with our relationship. Most of the time I feel left out—it isn't the way I want it to be, and I don't think it ever will be."

Alice indicated that she had a "very close" relationship with her older daughter, Amy. "We can talk about anything. At times I feel I unload too much about my unhappiness on her—it can't be good for her—and yet I can only talk with her or mother, and I need to have an outlet."

Mike and Alice did not have much social life. They rarely entertained at home, and most activities outside the house revolved around the children's activities. They were always present at the high school and junior high school athletic events where Amy was on the drill team and Harold played football and baseball.

In making decisions and solving problems, Mike usually had the final word. He paid the bills and managed the family's investments. Alice received a household allowance and, after some years of conflict, had resigned herself to Mike's firm policy that she had to manage on that amount. They both acknowledged, however, overspending on the children. "It's the only thing he ever gives in on—where he can really be softhearted," Alice said. She deferred to his opinions on most matters, and only occasionally did she appear angry about the scant influence she seemed to have. "Alice is not very good with money—forgets to fill out check stubs, doesn't keep an accurate balance and, in general, spends money impulsively. I had to take the responsibility away from her and put her on an allowance, and it works fine now."

The children appeared to be doing well. At 16, Amy was pretty and well-developed. She was an A student, on the drill team, and active in school affairs. She had not begun to date, however, and expressed little interest in boys. "They're all immature and I'm not interested." She was poised but somewhat shy. Amy felt that her father was the boss in the family, and that her relationship with Mother was the closer of the two. She was interested in biology and chemistry, and thought she might want to be a doctor. There was no suggestion of psychiatric symptoms such as fears, anxiety, or depression. She appeared to be the most self-controlled of the children.

Harold, at 14, was more outgoing and spontaneous. A large and well-developed boy without any hint of adolescent awkwardness, he moved with the easy coordination of an athlete. He was obviously popular with his peers and enjoyed doing a variety of things with boyfriends. He did not date, but admitted that he was "kind of going with" a neighborhood girl. He made B's and C's in school, and seemed satisfied with those grades. There was no evidence of significant emotional problems. Harold appeared to be a comfortable, symptom-free adolescent with considerable self-esteem and much in the way of social skills.

Susan, at 12, was outgoing, friendly, and described by other family members as "always happy." She had not yet developed sexually and, in talking with the interviewer, expressed impatience. "My friends have developed and are having periods and I feel funny to be the last one to start." Susan had many friends —"more than all the rest of us," according to Amy—and was constantly on the go. She was a good student and usually made A's. Her approach to school was somewhat haphazard. "Susan is bright," her father told the interviewer, "but terribly lacking in self-discipline. She does well without much effort, and I worry a little about that."

Although each child was different, they all appeared to be doing well. The professionals who interviewed them rated them as healthy, and psychological tests confirmed these opinions.

When the family was observed as a unit, many strengths were obvious. They cared for and were considerate of each other. They communicated with spontaneity. There was no difficulty understanding them, and each spoke his or her mind clearly. In solving problems, Mike took firm control of the family discussion and, although obviously interested in the others' ideas, appeared to come to a solution that was his own rather than a family consensus. As a family, there was some avoidance of showing feelings. In particular, there appeared to be a rule that forbade the open expression of anger. At times, this gave the family a muted quality. Mike and Alice did not talk about their relationship in front of the children, and seemed to keep the focus on events in the children's lives.

In a discussion of family problems, the theme was that they were without any real problems in comparison with other families. If one of the children attempted to bring up a family problem, one of the parents diverted the conversation to one of the neighbors' recent family misfortunes.

The Fortrans are representative of faltering families. They just miss being a healthy family. There is pain in the family that is not being dealt with. Alice seems to carry the family pain although, in his quiet way, Mike, too, has a share of it. The pain springs from their shared failure to evolve a relationship that has any real intimacy in it. At first glance, this appears to be more Mike's responsibility than it is Alice's. He is deeply reserved, avoids exposing feelings, and has strong needs to be in control of himself and others. Alice, however, has participated in this failure. She has not helped Mike to be more open, but has retreated into bitterness. There is an unhappy, sour quality to her, and increasingly she has turned to both her mother and Amy for intimate communication. She feels hopeless at times about her ever "getting enough" and sees clearly Mike's remoteness, but is blind to the many ways she contributes to their distant relationship.

The children seem to be healthy and doing well. Whether the underlying parental conflict will influence their choices of mates and the nature of their marriages is unknown. All that can be said is that they are doing well at the present.

In some ways, families like the Fortrans are most fortunate. They have achieved economic security, some of what is called success in this culture. The children are doing well. From the outside, they look like a very strong family. In other ways, however, the Fortrans can be seen as a tragic family. Tragic in the sense that, despite their strengths and success, they miss achieving what healthy families reveal is possible. Real intimacy is lacking and, because of this lack, there is a barely hidden undercurrent of disappointment, loneliness, and anger.

XI

Troubled Families

All families have troubles. Life brings a share of pain and misery to all of us. For some families troubles are occasional events, something to be dealt with. When no distressing issue is at hand, the family is not troubled, and life goes well. Other families, however, are troubled even when there is no particular distressing event—being troubled is part of the day-in and day-out business of living. These are troubled families.

At first glance, troubled families appear to be very different from each other. Each seems to be unique, and it is difficult to find any similarities. However, there are common patterns, and they can be understood if one knows what to look for. The healthy families in Chapter VIII were described along the following dimensions:

1) the parental marriage
2) power
3) closeness
4) communication
5) problem-solving
6) feelings
7) dealing with loss
8) family values
9) intimacy and autonomy

These factors, in combination, were correlated strongly with the health of the family—that is, how well a given family accomplished the two important tasks of supporting parental growth and raising healthy children. They are useful also in understanding troubled families. When such families are understood from the vantage point of these nine factors, similarities and patterns emerge. Three groups of troubled families become apparent. These are:

1) dominated families
2) conflicted families
3) chaotic families

Two of the groups, the dominated and conflicted families, can be either moderately or severely disturbed. The third group, chaotic families, are invariably severely disturbed. It is important to emphasize that all troubled families contain much pain and are disturbed, either in terms of producing autonomous children, or protecting the mental health of the parents, or both. Those families that fail to accomplish both are, by definition, severely disturbed families.

Before describing these three groups of families, it is important also to re-emphasize the continuum of family competence. The continuum would now look like this:

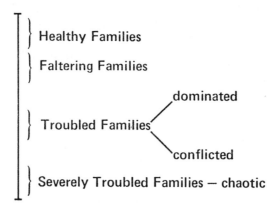

DOMINATED FAMILIES

These families are controlled and dominated, usually by one powerful parent. The parental relationship is clearly one of dominance and submission. One partner—most often the husband, but occasionally the wife—exerts all the power. His or her expertise extends into every area of life, and he or she has the final authority on any subject. The powerful one's control and authority can be absolute or, in some families, very dominant. In either event, the submissive spouse may either expect, even relish, the child-like position, or be angered by it and strike back in a variety of indirect ways. He or she may enter a coalition with a child, his or her own parent, or someone outside the family. In part, this appears to represent the general tendency of oppressed persons to seek a defense against the oppressor, but it may reflect also a search for intimacy, because intimacy is rare in dominant-submissive relationships. It is difficult for either the dominant or the submissive person to risk the deeper disclosures that are the heart of intimate communication.

If one sees that a family is dominated by one person, it is helpful to assess whether the domination is more-or-less accepted by the spouse and other members of the family, or whether there is active conflict and rebellion. Some dominated families have a relatively stable structure with little open conflict, whereas others involve daily strife as other family members rebel, undercut, and maneuver against the heavy-handed control of the dominant member.

One consequence of the dominated family is reduced opportunity for closeness. No one can get close to the dominant parent, for he or she cannot tolerate the vulnerability that closeness may suggest. Further, if the dominant parent is reasonably successful in the control of the family, there is often a general or widespread disinclination to be close. The focus of all relationships becomes power—who has the upper hand—rather than intimacy. It is as if the dominant parent sets the tone or style for the whole family.

Family communication and problem-solving clearly reflect the dominant parent's use of power. That can range from crude, raw domination to a subtle, hidden use of power. In either circumstance, there is little negotiating and little opportunity for children to learn directly the skills needed to find consensus, to compromise, or to differ agreeably.

These families do communicate clearly, however, and there is little difficulty knowing what individuals think. There is a strong tendency to avoid individual responsibility in these families. The feared displeasure or wrath of the dominant parent pushes others to hedge, avoid, or blame. On some occasions, a family scapegoat emerges who more-or-less accepts the blame for everything bad that happens.

There is some loss of permeability in the family. Individuals intent on dealing with a powerful person in the family are often so preoccupied with protecting themselves that they cannot develop a sensitive ear for other family members' messages. In addition, since it is risky to respond casually, there is very little spontaneous communication.

To express feelings is dangerous in a dominated family. To be angry, upset, hurt, or sad often leads to disapproval. In many such families, there is a constant undercurrent of resentment towards the powerful parent—but it would be foolhardy to express it openly. Such unexpressed feelings frequently find an outlet in rebellious behavior out of the sight of the dominant person or by being converted to sadness and depression. Any surviving affection and joy are muted.

Such families do not deal well with change, in particular the loss of someone or something cared about. These families are so rigidly controlled that there is less of the flexibility which is necessary to deal with change and loss. Rigid rules prevail, and many such families are organized around authoritarian value systems. These beliefs dictate what is right or wrong, and they must be followed regardless of circumstances. The dominant parent makes the rules and is both the prosecutor and judge when others deviate from them.

Dominated families are not settings for the growth of intimacy, and often make the achievement of autonomy difficult. Growing up in such a family, one learns to be wary of closeness and gradually becomes accustomed to having someone else make all the decisions. Sometimes children leave these families at an early age. "I married at 16 to get away from home." Others cling dependently to the powerful parent, while some rebel actively and often carry excessive problems in dealing with other authority figures into adulthood.

Dominated families often produce one or more psychiatric patients. Although what causes any individual to develop mental or emotional illness always involves other factors (such as heredity, childhood experiences, or social deprivation), growing up or living in a family dominated by one individual increases the likelihood of breakdown. In such a setting, it is not easy to learn to be comfortable with intimate communication, to accept mistakes as part of being human, to feel good about one's self and others; it poses stresses every-day, and rarely provides adults with the emotional support so neces-sary in times of difficulty.

Clinically, one sees a variety of individual symptoms: excessively inhibited, shy, or withdrawn persons, impulsive rebels always in trouble with authorities, people who are depressed or fearful, and fragile individuals who crumble under stress.

Connie, a 15-year-old girl, was referred to a psychiatrist be-cause of excessive and increasing fears. Since the age of 13 she had developed a number of phobias. At first these had involved heights, but they gradually included any room where there were more than a few people. For several months prior to the referral, she had refused to leave her bedroom and took all her meals there. As part of Connie's evaluation, the entire family was seen.

The family interview was completely dominated by the father, a successful surgeon. He took complete charge, asked all the questions, ordered members of the family to answer, cut off their responses at will, changed the subject frequently, and was sarcastic and openly demeaning to his wife. Connie's mother was passive, subdued, and mouse-like in appearance. She sat close to Connie and held her hand. Jeff, the 19-year-old son, was sullen and appeared very angry. He had not made his grades in college and had been home and unable to find a job for six months. This displeased his father, who had threatened to "kick him out of the house."

The father's style was open and overbearing domination. The mother had entered into a coalition with Connie and spent much time with Connie in her room. Jeff, too, was caught up in the family dilemma and seemed to make a point of behavior that displeased his father.

In individual interviews, it was apparent that each member of the family was in great pain. Connie was fearful, crying, and obviously depressed. Psychologically, she seemed abnormally de-pendent on her mother. Jeff was angry and critical of his father. He seemed unaware of any connection between his frequent failures and the anger at his father. The mother was quiet, depressed, and talked about a deep feeling of loneliness. The father was angry and bitter about the way his family was turning out. He said that he had to "carry" them all and felt burdened about his inability to make things better. He saw his dominant and controlling behavior as a response to the other family members' inadequacies.

This family is representative of the pattern of dominated families. All members are victimized by the nature of the relationships they have evolved. Each participates in its perpetuation and sees only that which the others do, all the while remaining blind to his or her contribution. This mutually destructive way of being a family started with the parents' marriage and the parents' shared need to effect a dominant-submissive relationship. Although each denied knowing prior to the marriage that the other was either dominant or submissive, both were subsequently found to be repeating the marital pattern that had existed in their parents' relationships.

This type of troubled family makes up a large percentage of the families from which psychiatric patients emerge. Even when there are no patients, this way of being a family is associated with a good deal of pain. It fails by a considerable margin to achieve the best possible in being a family.

CONFLICTED FAMILIES

Conflicted families present a very different pattern from the dominated families. Parents are unable to share power, and each struggles openly to control the other. Since neither is willing to accept a submissive role, there is constant warfare. The effect of the struggle and competition upon the family is considerable and destructive.

The parents can never decide who has the right to make which decisions. They cannot evolve a stable set of rules about power, authority, and responsibility and, as a consequence, each continues to seek control. Tension, manipulativeness, sarcasm, and attempts to involve others in the struggle are common. The relationship seems based on conflict as if there would be nothing without the warfare. Certainly there is no intimacy, for sharing provides the other with new ammunition for the next attack.

Coalitions are common, but often fleeting in nature. Children are drawn into the marital conflict, first on one side, then the other. Occasionally, a stable parent-child alliance emerges and the child comes to see one parent as "good" and the other as "bad." The parents of the marital couple are often involved as allies for their child. Closer outside relationships evolve, often a "best friend" who accepts the husband's or wife's account of the endless conflicts as factual and becomes a co-conspirator. The absence of intimacy in such marriages, coupled with unrelenting anger, sets the stage for extramarital affairs.

The whole family suffers from the parental power struggle. There is little other than the conflict that is enduring. Children, often drawn to one side or the other, grow up in an atmosphere where power is all important and conflicts anticipated. There is little in the parents' relationship to provide a model for closeness, and relationships within the family become cautious and distant.

Communications are usually clear, but efficiency in problem-solving is diminished because disagreements, rather than leading to negotiation, often are but the initial stage of an escalating attack-counterattack between the parents. Blaming others is common, and there is little to encourage individual family members to accept the responsibility for their own thoughts, feelings, and behavior. Nevertheless, many conflicted families develop high levels of permeability. Knowing and acknowledging what others have said is important because it may represent the start of a new attack or provide a weapon with which to attack others.

Angry feelings are freely expressed, but "softer" feelings like affection, sadness, or tenderness are masked or avoided because they may place one in a vulnerable position. These families, with such high levels of anger, often do not deal well with loss. Guilt may follow the loss of someone seen as on the "other side," and vulnerability or fear may follow the loss of an ally.

Family values are often intensely competitive. Winning is the name of the game, and frequently anything is justified to achieve victory.

Children growing up in this kind of family usually achieve reasonable levels of autonomy, but are not good candidates for adult intimacy. Closeness is not easily learned in conflicted families. These families also produce psychiatric patients, particularly children with serious behavior disturbances and adults who develop depression in midlife.

> The Custers sought professional help regarding their 14-year-old son, Chip. When they called, they indicated that he was failing in school, had been picked up by the police for vandalism, hung around with a group of "delinquents," and was probably using drugs. They were asked to have their 17-year-old daughter and Chip come with them for the initial evaluation appointment. At that time, Chip was seen individually, the parents were interviewed together, and the family interviewed together.
>
> Realistically, Chip was involved in alarming, pre-delinquent behavior; however, the family as a whole was seriously troubled, and Chip's behavior was, in part, a reflection of that disturbance. In the family interview, the intense and longstanding conflict between the parents surfaced immediately. Mrs. Custer, an aggressive person, openly attacked her husband for his rigid, punitive attitude toward Chip. He, in turn, was sarcastic and critical of her for "babying and protecting" Chip. Chip was silent and sullen during this interchange, obviously caught between his warring parents. He was mother's ally in her battle and seemed to be a very exasperating adversary for the father, who was unable to direct or control Chip. The parents' hostile dialogue soon moved away from Chip and focused on each other's deficiencies. Mrs. Custer accused her husband of being weak, detached, and tied to his mother's apron strings. He, in turn, suggested that she was an aggressive, conniving, unfeminine bitch. The marital conflict precluded any serious or sustained attention to the very real problems posed by Chip's behavior.
>
> Carol, the 17-year-old daughter, was a silent and disdainful bystander. She sat in a chair as far removed from the other members of the family as possible. In answering the questions as to how she saw the family problem, she stated clearly that the whole family was "badly messed up," and that she wished only to leave for college or to get married, or "something."

This family is an example of many conflicted families. The constant warfare brings pain to all. The parents lead lives that, in many ways, have a bitter and desperate quality. The children are either dragged into the conflict or early in life give up hope of finding happiness within the family and begin to distance themselves from the tragic scene.

CHAOTIC FAMILIES

Chaotic families fail miserably to achieve the two basic tasks of the family. They are often severely disorganized and isolated from the outside world, and may appear "strange" or "bizarre" to those who come in contact with them.

The parents' relationship is invariably severely distressed. One pattern is the fused marriage. The couple is joined together in a way that obliterates individuality. Husband and wife must always have the same opinion, think the same, and feel alike. Any hint of individual thoughts or feelings may be experienced as desertion. There is a "weness" that is malignant to any sense of personal uniqueness. A second pattern is that of the burned-out marriage in which emotional divorce has occurred long ago; there is no life remaining, and yet the couple cling together, making do with their emptiness. Coalitions with the parents' families of origin are frequent. Often, one or both sets of grandparents live next door or nearby.

No one has enough power to structure the family and the result is chaos. Sometimes these families will be seen with a chronically disturbed child—often an adolescent—and it is not rare to find that the very sick youngster has more influence than anyone else in the family. The family clings together and sometimes resembles a glob of protoplasm in which the observer has difficulty knowing what each individual feels and thinks.

Communication is difficult to follow and the flow of ideas in a family conversation and meaning are thus obscured. Often members appear not to hear each other; at other times, they seem to use a private language. Problems are often totally disregarded. A child's mental illness may be brushed aside with, "It's only nervousness—it will disappear," until outsiders point out hallucinations, delusions, or bizarre behavior. Feelings are frequently denied and some chaotic families have a flat, monotonous quality. The prevailing family mood may involve despair, hopelessness, or cynicism.

These families have a difficult time dealing with any change. Adolescents are treated as if they were nursery-school age, and parental aging is denied. Losses, in particular, are often completely denied. The reality of someone's death, for example, is simply not acknowledged, and the family may continue to behave as if the person were still alive. This, along with the other characteristics, gives many of these families an eerie, spooky quality. Their shared reality is not that of most others.

Chaotic families discourage individuality, independence, autonomy, and change. One is not expected to grow up and leave—it is as if life is changeless and death does not occur. Nor do these families provide the emotional support necessary to sustain individuals through crises. While chaotic families represent only a small fraction of families seen in clinical practice, they often include one or more members with severe mental illnesses. In particular, this type of family is associated with chronic, severe illness in which the individual's thinking is severely disorganized, out of touch with reality, and often bizarre.

The Gordons were referred by the probate court after their 21-year-old daughter, Esther, had been picked up by the police for walking nude down the suburban street on which the family lived. The charges against Esther were dropped when the family agreed to seek private psychiatric care. When the family brought her for evaluation, it quickly became apparent that Esther was severely disturbed. She thought that she was the Virgin Mary. Her speech was incoherent at times, she rambled in a disconnected manner, and for the most part it was difficult to follow her thinking. Her parents seemed unalarmed and were themselves difficult to understand. Mrs. Gordon indicated that Esther had always been "a little nervous," to which her husband responded, "well, everyone is." They seemed unmindful of her plight, talking in a disconnected way about the police officer who had taken her into custody, the judge who had insisted on treatment for her, the neighborhood in which they lived, and other subjects that appeared to relate only tenuously to their daughter's condition.

Gradually, a picture of the family emerged: Mr. Gordon, a postal supervisor, was a painfully shy and solitary man, having only two important relationships, his wife and Esther. Mrs. Gordon was equally reclusive, relating only to her husband, Esther, and her own parents, who lived next door. She and her mother had an unusually close relationship. They shopped together, planned menus together, and Mrs. Gordon never bought clothes without her mother's approval.

Esther had not been planned for and, in fact, the Gordons had decided not to have children. Since infancy, however, Mrs. Gordon had been "very close" to Esther, who was a quiet, shy, and withdrawn child. She did not play with other children, had great difficulty separating from her mother to attend first grade, and had developed into a shy, withdrawn teenager. She graduated from high school, but refused to go to college or to work. She stayed at home with her mother and grandmother each day. As well as can be determined, the onset of her serious disturbance occurred when her mother experienced a severe episode of flu, and Esther thought she might die.

The Gordons were little known in their neighborhood, and were considered a "strange" family. As far as could be determined, no neighbor had ever been in their home.

This family illustrates the most serious level of family disturbance known to professionals. The Gordon's failure to produce clearly individualized family members, their denial of reality, the extreme social withdrawal, and their chaotic pattern of communicating, when considered together, produce a human network in which emotional support is minimal and autonomy next to impossible. To live in such a family may limit terribly the degree to which one grows to one's human potential.

These three distinct patterns of troubled families—the dominated, the conflicted, and the chaotic—stand in sharp contrast to healthy families and are different from faltering families. They represent failures in the search for what is possible in human relationships. For the family members involved, life often contains far more pain and misery than it does satisfaction and joy.

XII

Family Stress

All families must deal with stress; there is no escaping it, although there is enormous variation in the amount of stress different families are called upon to face. How well a family does so is an important aspect of its overall competence.

There are several important aspects of stress. One concerns whether it is acute or chronic. Acute stress usually comes as the result of a sudden, unpleasant occurrence: a son is expelled from school, a father loses his job, a mother is found to have cancer, or a daughter is hurt in an automobile accident. Most often, the stress results from an unanticipated event which threatens the continuation of the family life as it had been before the event occurred. Such sudden, unforeseen stress occurs in all families.

In contrast to acute stress is stress that is present day after day, month after month. Although it may have started suddenly and been severe, when it becomes chronic—rather than a limited episode—it is like a cloud that settles upon the family, and it has an entirely different impact. Protracted illness, poverty, prejudice, and uncertain living circumstances are examples.

A second aspect of family stress is whether its source is internal or external. Internal family stress results from faulty relationships, parents who are chronically conflicted, a family rigidly dominated by one member, or a child whose behavior is counter to the family's values.

External family stress is strain that originates outside the family, but has a direct and painful influence on the family. The death of a close friend, a business failure, or social unrest in one's neighborhood are examples.

A third feature regarding family stress involves whether or not something specific can be done about it. Some types of stress have such a focused and clearly defined source that the difficulty can be seen as clear, understandable, and definable. Families are more apt to be able to function well because, however, severe the strain, their course of action is usually clear. In contrast, some kinds of stress are diffuse and harder to understand, and there is great uncertainty about how to operate in the circumstances. Broad economic changes such as depression or runaway inflation are examples of this type of stress.

These factors obviously overlap, but considering the various components of stress—whether it is acute or chronic, internal or external, and clear or uncertain—can be helpful in understanding a family's attempts to deal with it. Although there is considerable variation from family to family, stress that is experienced as clear, acute, and external is often the easiest to handle.

Another factor to be considered involves whether or not a family's initial attempts to cope with stress are successful in blunting its initial impact or, in themselves, add to the strain. This notion that a family's initial response either alleviates or increases the stress is of great importance because often a family can do little about the stress itself. This is particularly so in dealing with external stress. The death of a loved one, serious illness in a family member, or severe racial prejudice are examples of the type of stress that is inescapable. However, their initial responses often can be modified in ways that make the situation less stressful. Much of the work of professionals in what is called "crisis intervention" attempts to assist families to deal with emergencies in ways that do not add to the struggle.

John, the seven-year-old son of Horace and Estelle Brown, was admitted to the burn unit of a hospital with third-degree burns over his abdomen, back, and legs. There was real question whether he would survive but, even under the best of circumstances, he was facing a long period of hospitalization.

The psychiatric consultant to the unit was asked to see the

family because the nurses had noted that for several days the parents and two older sons sat silently in the waiting room at some distance from each other. They did not talk with each other, and each of them stared blankly into space.

The consultant pieced together the following clinical facts: Horace, a successful engineer, was a "strong," outspoken man who tended to dominate the family. He made most family decisions and was seen by the others as capable, powerful, and rarely, if ever, wrong. He was not, however, the type of man who shared his feelings easily. Estelle and the three sons were somewhat in awe of him, and he seemed to serve as the family model of what a strong and good person should be.

John, the youngest son, was seen as "special" in the family. He was considered to be the brightest of the three boys, well coordinated, and with both athletic promise and considerable musical talent.

The threat of John's death was so frightening to the family that they were unable to talk about it. The family members looked to Horace for leadership in facing this painful possibility, and he seemed unable to respond openly. As a consequence, each family member was terribly alone with his or her fears. There was no being together, and each person's fear was intensified by the isolation.

The consultant spent some time with Horace and was able to help him face openly the fear of John's death. Horace was encouraged to share his fear and sense of helplessness with the family. The consultant met with the family and encouraged the open sharing of each individual's fears. The results were dramatic. After a 20- or 30-minute family session in which everyone cried and expressed an individual sense of responsibility for John's accident, the family sat closer together, talked with each other, and seemed much more a family under severe stress rather than four individuals alone with severe stress. Horace was able to provide leadership to the family by assigning each individual certain responsibilities and devising a schedule that allowed each family member to spend time alone with John.

In this family, a terrible stress was increased by the family's initial response. There was no coming together and sharing of individual fears and sense of helplessness. As a consequence, each person had to deal with the stress alone and without the comfort the family could provide.

Internal stress can lead also to initial reactions that increase the family stress.

> Marshall and Claudia Wingate had been married 11 years and had two daughters. They had not worked out a satisfactory solution to the issue of power. Each was an aggressive person and sought to dominate the other. As a consequence, their relationship involved frequent disagreements about who had the right to do what. It seemed to make no difference what the specific issue was—buying a car, planning a vacation, or what to have for dinner—each decision the family faced led to a battle.
>
> The two daughters had come to expect daily conflicts as a part of family life. When the parental conflict reached a certain level, both Marshall and Claudia withdrew, often for several days. Claudia retreated to the bedroom, went to bed, and either slept or read. Marshall did not come home from work until the daughters were asleep, and he left early each morning. During these "cooling off" periods, neither parent prepared meals or in any way concerned themselves with the children's needs.

Although their separate retreats may have blunted the intense conflict, it increased the strain for the daughters. They felt abandoned, convinced that they were not loved, and that the family was on the brink of dissolution. The parents' efforts to reduce conflict increased rather than eased the stress for their children.

An important mitigation of family stress is the presence of other support systems. Families who have close relationships with relatives or friends, or strong involvements with organizations like their church or fellow workers, can receive help and cope more easily with stressful situations. Those families who are more isolated and must face stress without such support usually are less competent.

STRESS AND THE LEVEL OF
FAMILY COMPETENCE

In previous chapters, the advantages of being able to locate families on a continuum of family competence was emphasized. Healthy families are at one end of the continuum. Next, one finds faltering families, then troubled families of either the dominated or conflicted types and, at the lowest level of competence, severely troubled or chaotic families. The characteristics of families at different levels of competence were described. In a somewhat simplified way, this continuum of structure can be seen as moving from flexible (healthy families) to rigid (troubled families) to chaotic (severely troubled families) processes. This progression, flexible → rigid → chaotic, is important in understanding a family's response to stress for two reasons. First, each level is associated with certain responses to stress. Second, if a family at a certain level of competence is unable to deal with the stress, the family structure will move toward the next lower level of functioning. Flexible families will move toward rigidity, rigid families to chaos, and the chaotic families, already disorganized, show no movement because they are already at the lowest level. One may see, however, an increase in the family's baseline level of hopelessness and despair.

Healthy Families and Stress

Healthy families do not have to contend with the chronic, internal stress that grows out of poor family relationships. This gives such families freedom from feeling overwhelmed by difficulty. They are in a position to use all their strengths and skills in coping with stress. Their expertise in living includes excellent problem-solving abilities and an approach to problems (including stress) that gives even small difficulties immediate attention. Their openness to each family member's perceptions and opinions leads to clarification and the possibility of a shared reality. They can seek general agreement about the nature of the stress and everyone can play a part in the effort to deal with it.

Because healthy families share power, their ability to cope with stress is not dependent on the skills of a single individual. The cliché, "two heads (or more) are better than one," applies. Parents provide effective leadership, and children are a part of the joint effort to deal with stressful circumstances.

The openness of healthy families to the expression of feelings is a distinct advantage in dealing with stress. Each member of the family knows where the others are emotionally, and anxiety, sadness, fear, or other emotions are accepted as part of a truly human response to a difficult situation.

Finally, these families do not quickly settle for a simple "solution."

They seem to appreciate complexities, and take the time to explore a number of possibilities. Once a plan of action has been agreed upon, the family moves into action. If the situation cannot be changed or, at the minimum, the intensity of the experienced stress reduced, healthy families re-examine the situation and search for a new understanding. It is this trial-and-error flexibility that characterizes the healthy family's attempts to deal with stress. In addition, the family is apt to feel that they face life together rather than alone, and they share responsibility. In this way, no individual is overburdened, each is supported and important, and children learn a process that applies to solving problems of all kinds.

> The Crow family faced the sudden and unanticipated loss of the father's job as a foreman in an electronics company. The father's job had been terminated as part of a sudden cutback secondary to the loss of a government contract. It had come with little warning, despite the father's 11 years of productive work for that company.
> Jack, the father, called his wife from the plant, shared the bad news with her, and they quickly decided to discuss it with the children that evening. At that time, their 14-year-old son became angry and upset, and their 11-year-old daughter cried. The parents did not try to blunt or stifle those feelings but, rather, shared some of their own concerns and anxieties. Following this, the family discussed a number of alternatives. Jack pointed out that their savings, plus the termination pay, would carry them for four or five months. They discussed ways of economizing, and each family member had something to offer. The long-range uncertainties, including the possibility of moving to a different part of the country in which the economy was less depressed, were discussed.

The children felt well informed and very much a part of the search for solutions. The feelings precipitated by the stress were shared and considered natural. Jack received considerable support from his family. No one felt alone because no one was excluded from knowledge of or a share in the solution of what was truly a family event beyond their control. As serious as it was, they could feel competent to deal with it.

Faltering Families and Stress

Faltering families, less able than healthy but more effective than troubled families, often have considerable skills with which to deal with stress. The internal stress in the parents' marriage is experienced primarily by the wife and does not permeate every aspect of family life. In this sense, the dysfunction is more or less confined, leaving considerable energy available to deal with stress—particularly if it is acute, external, and clearly defined.

Many faltering families have reasonably open communication and considerable skill with which to solve problems. They can share and clarify the nature of the stress, but are less prone to share feelings, and this may lead to each member's feeling alone. It is as if faltering families have many of the features that allow optimal families to cope with stress, but defects in the parental relationship lead to strong feelings which are not openly expressed. This interferes with the whole family's capacity to be open with feelings of all types.

There is a strong tendency for these families to become more rigid and dominated under stress. Most often, the detached father moves into a controlling and directive position, and the coping with the stress more clearly reflects his skill than it does the functioning of the family as a whole. As will be described later, this may have real advantage to the family if the stress is severe and threatens to result in family disorganization or chaos.

Mary and Bill had three children, a good family reputation, and a marriage that left Mary chronically unhappy. Bill was a sales executive, traveled a great deal, and when he was at home was quiet, preoccupied, and involved in many solitary hobbies. Mary was obese, and had mild colitis, and focused most of her energy on their three children.

Bill's job was threatened when the company he worked for was absorbed by a larger, out-of-state corporation. He was told that his company's products would be handled by the larger corporation's sales force and that it was not known whether or not he would have a job. He was to be informed of the final decision within 60 days.

Bill did not tell Mary or the children, but brooded about it, became even more detached, and very irritable. After ten days, Mary confronted him with the intolerable conditions she experienced and, in the midst of an angry scene, he explained the uncertainty of their economic future. They were able to discuss possible solutions, which included searching for a new job, going into business with Mary's father, or, if offered, accepting a job with the larger corporation even if it meant a move to a different part of the country. They disagreed about discussing it with the children. "No use to upset them" was Bill's theme, and "They know something is wrong and have a right to know what it is" was Mary's argument. Her views prevailed, and the source of the family stress was clarified. What was not permitted, however, was any discussion of feelings. Bill did not share his concerns and fears of an uncertain future, and when Mary tried to express her feelings, he quickly shifted the subject to the facts. As a consequence, each family member was alone with his or her feelings.

This type of family can survive most forms of stress because their strengths and skills outweigh their limitations. Nevertheless, their restricted capacity to deal with stress in a more open and flexible manner leaves the members lonely, frightened, and hurt.

Troubled Families and Stress

Troubled families are characterized by rigidity. Whether the pattern is one of domination or open conflict, there is a "stuck-in-one-gear" quality that robs such families of flexibility. These families respond repeatedly with a stereotyped response. Then, when the single gear fails, the family becomes increasingly disorganized. Like any rigid structure, when the capacity to deal with stress is exceeded, fragmentation occurs.

The dominated family is at risk to the extent and in the ways that the dominant family member is vulnerable. His or her strengths may carry the family through a stressful period. If, however, he or she cannot manage without the support of others, the inability to use others' strengths may prove crucial.

Furthermore, many dominated families have underlying, hidden conflicts with resulting internal stress. This may drain the family of the energy needed to deal with additional stress. These families rarely are open to the expression of feelings and, even if the skills of the dominant member are sufficient to cope with the stress, family members must often deal with their feelings alone.

Dominated members of these families often feel like children with one powerful parent. This rarely results in the development of either confidence or the practiced skills useful in coping with stress.

Conflicted families are even less likely to cope adequately with significant stress. The parents' conflict is so pervasive that even dreadfully stressful situations are apt to be grasped by one parent to be used as a weapon against the other. In some families, one parent is able to achieve control and dominance during a stressful period, but is unable to maintain it when the crisis has passed.

Many troubled families deny the real source of the stress and assign responsibility either to one family member, the scapegoat, or to outsiders. This search for a simple sort of understanding—"It's Mary, she causes all the trouble," or "It's the Blacks (Jews, Catholics, 'them')"—is a common theme in troubled families. Such oversimplification and blaming result in the failure to clarify and understand the source of the stress and subsequently, lead to a failure to explore various approaches to coping with stress.

> The Hintons were a tightly controlled military family. Al Hinton, a career officer, ruled his family in the rigid, rule-oriented manner he did his troops. Punishment, rather than reward, played a major role in the family. His wife, Ruth, was childlike in her dependency upon him. The four children were inhibited, withdrawn, and unusually subservient. Al made the rules and the decisions, and he solved every problem the family faced.
>
> The particular stress for this family was precipitated by the passing over of Al for promotion. This event threatened his military career and made the family's future uncertain. For the other family members, the event was incomprehensible. Al was seen as all-powerful and incapable of error. The notion that anyone could find him lacking in any way was unbelievable.
>
> Al was overwhelmed by this unexpected stress. He appeared confused and irrational for several days. Later, he became depressed and was unable to function. As this occurred, the family began to fall apart. The family dictator was unable to maintain control; Ruth appeared even more helpless than usual, and soon took her to bed; the children seemed lost and without direction.

The family seemed to drift through the days, and even meals were not prepared.

Al began to think that a group of Catholic officers had plotted against him out of jealousy and had influenced the promotion decision. He talked incessantly about this, and Ruth and the children accepted it as the truth. Gradually, the family achieved some semblance of structure—all of which centered about their now shared belief that "the Catholics plotted against Father." Al retired from the service, and the family returned to Ruth's family's farm.

This troubled family was incapable of dealing realistically with this particular stress. The inability of the father to accept being passed over led to a period of disorganization and chaos from which the family emerged through projecting the responsibility on an outside group. This distortion of reality was shared by the whole family, and resulted in cessation of other and potentially more effective coping devices. The projection or "paranoid" family stance did, however, aid the family in emerging from the chaos in which they were imbedded.

Severely Troubled Families and Stress

As one moves down the continuum of family competence, families have fewer skills with which to deal with stress. Healthy families have more than faltering families who, in turn, have more than troubled families. At the lowest level of competence are chaotic families, and they have the least number of skills to use in dealing with stress. Their basic disorganization precludes any realistic appraisal of the causes of the difficulty. Chaotic families rely on denial of reality, refusing to accept the way the world is; in their shared distortions they often come to bizarre conclusions. Often, when an acute problem is added to the chronic, severe, internal strains of such families, one notes even greater disorganization and deepening despair.

The Turners were a strange and eccentric family. The father, Ray, was a certified public accountant who was quiet and meticulous. Sue, his wife, was an erratic woman who had been hospitalized repeatedly for periods of confusion. During these periods, she became delusional and thought that she was a special messenger from another planet. Their two daughters were very different. Ellen was disorganized and had been hospitalized twice for confused episodes. Jane was meticulous, withdrawn, and rarely initiated any relationships.

The family physician had noted that the family was difficult to understand, rarely sought medical attention unless severely ill, and frequently did not follow simple instructions or take the medications prescribed.

This terribly limited family was further stressed by an automobile accident in which the father was injured. He required lengthy hospitalization, but had no economic reserves, no hospitalization insurance, and an accounting business that barely produced a living for the family. Under these distressing circumstances, the family became even more dysfunctional. Both the mother and the older daughter soon required psychiatric hospitalization, and Jane went to live with her grandparents. The family had no reserves either of skill or money, and it literally fell apart.

The fragile quality of these unfortunate families is often noted by others. Family members may cling together in a way that obliterates their individuality. There is rarely a strong individual who may carry the family through the stress. Often these families disintegrate or become dependent upon the extended family or social agencies.

STRESS AND FAMILY GROWTH

Up to this point, the sole consideration has been on the destructive impact of stress on families of differing levels of competence. Under conditions of severe and prolonged stress, even the most competent families will suffer and move towards rigidity and, ultimately, chaos. Families with less competence will be handicapped by less severe stress.

There can be under certain circumstances, however, a positive aspect to family stress. For all but the least competent families, lesser amounts of stress may promote family growth. There is something about being exposed to some stress that jolts a family into reevaluating its skills and characteristic ways of dealing with life. Assets that are hidden or little used may be discovered. The sharing can lead to deeper appreciation of each individual's humanness. Family stereotypes may be shattered and myths dissolved. Coping successfully with stress can lead to increased family confidence in the ability to deal with future difficulties.

Arthur and Peggy Suttle and their two sons were a sturdy group. Arthur was the football coach at the local high school and tended to dominate his family subtly. Peggy, a competent teacher, consistently deferred to Arthur's judgment and enthusiasm. Both boys appeared to be doing well, but seemed somewhat afraid of their large and powerful father.

Arthur had a heart attack while jogging and almost died. Following a period of hospitalization, his recovery seemed assured. During his nearly fatal illness, Peggy ran the family with quiet competence. She made the necessary decisions and helped the boys to deal openly with their concerns and fears regarding Arthur's illness. When he returned home to convalesce, he attempted to resume his dominant role. Peggy, now accustomed to a different role in the family, refused to return to a position of subservience. This led to some conflict which Arthur and Peggy gradually resolved. As they did, it was with a much more equal distribution of power in which both of them had a hand in decision-making.

In this family, a serious stress resulted in family growth. They moved from a mildly dominated family to one with greater flexibility.

It is, of course, encouraging to see families grow as a result of stressful experiences. Stress is inevitable, and to realize that it does not invariably have destructive results upon the family offers hope that strength can emerge out of crisis.

XIII

Families and Physical Illness

In most neighborhoods there are families who seem to have a tremendous amount of physical illness and families who have very little.

The Smalley's have three children, a comfortable home, and reasonable economic security. On their street, they are thought of as a "strong" family. The children play with other children, do well in school and, on the surface, seem well-adjusted. The parents seem friendly, and often are the first to help those in need. Although no one in the neighborhood knows the Smalleys at an intimate level, from a distance they seem to be doing well.

However, a detailed medical history of the whole family would show that the family is having a large number and variety of illnesses. In the 17 years since the parents' marriage in 1960, the following illnesses have been experienced;

Mr. Smalley: pneumonia (1961), fractured ankle (1961), influenza requiring hospital care (1962), fractured wrist (1963), duodenal ulcer (1965), surgical removal of hemorrhoids (1967), fractured arm (1970), reoccurrence of duodenal ulcer (1972), surgical removal of gall bladder (1973), pneumonia (1975), and myocardial infarction ("heart attack") (1977).

Mrs. Smalley: influenza (1962), fractured arm (1963), surgical removal of ovarian cysts (1963), carcinoma of uterus with surgical removal (1973), pneumonia (1976).

The children: the two boys and one girl have experienced five fractures. One son has severe asthma and has been hospitalized five times (1969, 1970, 1972—2 times, 1973). Two of the children had acute appendicitis and subsequent appendectomies.

In 17 years, the family had 16 hospitalizations, in addition to those required by Mrs. Smalley's three pregnancies. Nine fractures and two life-threatening illnesses had been experienced, in addition to numerous upper-respiratory and gastrointestinal illnesses.

Across the street from the Smalleys live the Alton Jones family. They, too, have three children, a comfortable home, and reasonable economic security. Like the Smalleys, they are well-regarded in the neighborhood. The Jones family medical history, however, is very different from that of the Smalleys. There have been no life-threatening illnesses, no hospitalizations other than for Mrs. Jones's three pregnancies. One son fractured his ankle playing baseball. They have had only occasional upper-respiratory and gastrointestinal disturbances. The Jones family does not experience many illnesses—in fact, the 16 years of their family's existence have been remarkably healthy.

How can the difference between the physical health of the Smalleys and the Jones be understood? What are the factors that make these different patterns of health and illness so pronounced? Although science has not provided anything like a full understanding, there are some tantalizing leads and suggestions for future research.

Of course, the impact of heredity, nutrition, and other biologic factors must be acknowledged. There is no question that such factors play a role in family vulnerability or susceptibility to illness. However, those factors, in themselves, do not provide a thorough understanding; consideration must be given to the role of life experiences as they influence susceptibility to illness. This chapter will present a picture of the role of life circumstances as they relate to the development of physical illness in the family members.

As might be expected, there has been far more attention paid to the life circumstances of individuals and their relationship to illness than there has been to families. We're accustomed to thinking of illness as something individuals have and only think of the family as "having" illnesses if several individuals in the family are ill. Most studies of life circumstances and illness focus, therefore, on the individual rather than on illnesses within the family or family patterns of illness. The studies of individual life circumstances and their relationship to illness, however, can set the stage for a consideration of what is known about families and illness.

The studies of individuals and their life circumstances can be divided conveniently into four categories. These are:

1) Life change and illness
2) Life stress and illness
3) Loss and illness
4) Giving-up and illness

LIFE CHANGE AND ILLNESS

Illness is not distributed evenly in a population. At any economic level, there are some persons who have a great deal of illness and others who have practically none. Also, illnesses do not occur haphazardly, but tend to cluster in periods of six months or so. For example, an individual may have many months of freedom from all illness except minor colds or gastrointestinal upsets, then have two or three distinct and very different illnesses (a cluster) in a short time. The two or three illnesses are not related in the same sense that one is associated with another—they are understood as very different kinds of illnesses. This uneven distribution of illnesses in any population and the tendency for illnesses to cluster in time have encouraged scientists to look closely at what is going on in the lives of the individuals when illness begins.

One fascinating approach has focused on the amount of change in the lives of individuals during the months prior to the onset of illness. Although there are exceptions, individuals, on the average, are more prone to illness following a period of many life changes ranging from serious events like the death of a spouse to less serious events like changing jobs. On the basis of a study of a large number of people over an extended period, life events of different degrees of seriousness were given different "weights" so that it is possible to obtain a total life change score which reflects both the number and seriousness of an individual's life changes at any time.

One such study looked at the life changes of Naval personnel for the months prior to an extended period of sea duty. The sailors were divided into "high life-change" individuals and "low life-change" individuals. During the sea duty, there occurred an epidemic of serious dysentery—more sailors with high life-change scores developed this infection than those with low-life change scores.

It appears that, for many individuals, a period in which there is a great deal of change may be followed by increased susceptibility to illness.

LIFE STRESS AND ILLNESS

Although there is a general acceptance of the role of stress in increasing susceptibility to illness, this is a difficult area to study. Stress is a broad term, hard to measure, and very individualized. What is stressful for one person is not necessarily so for others.

One approach has been the attempt to correlate the onset of illness in individuals with periods of life stress. Questions have been raised, for example, regarding whether the increased susceptibility to illness in some persons following periods of high life change is not, in actuality, a reflection of the stress associated with life change. Other scientists have studied particular groups of individuals who are in difficult and stressful situations and noted that more such individuals develop a wide variety of illnesses than do individuals not in such stressful situations. Refugees struggling to adapt to a new country and recently promoted employees are examples of stressed populations. Another approach has been to contrast the frequency of illnesses in persons employed in stressful jobs with the frequency in those employed in nonstressful occupations. An example of this type of study would focus on airport control tower personnel who are stressed by the high level of vigilance required and small level of error permissible in such work.

LOSS AND ILLNESS

A number of studies suggest that some individuals are more prone to get sick in the months following the loss of a loved one. A stroll through a cemetery will reveal a surprising number of graves in which a couple have died within six or eight months of each other.

Studies of recently widowed persons reveal a higher risk of illness, hospitalization, and even death in the months following loss. Psychotherapists have noted in their patients the correlation between loss of a loved one and the development of either physical or mental illness. The loss of a loved one may be a particularly important life change and life stress that can, in some persons, increase susceptibility to illness.

GIVING UP AND ILLNESS

A major problem in studying the role of life circumstances in illness is the enormous variation among different persons in response to what appears to be an identical life circumstance. One man loses his wife and develops a severe depression, another develops cancer, and a third carves out a new life, often involving expanded interests and activities. This has led to the idea that it is not simply the life change, stress, or loss that is important, but how the individual copes with the circumstances.

An example of this point of view involves the observations about giving up. Doctors have noted that sick patients who give up often get worse, even die. Prisoner-of-war observations suggest the same thing. Prisoners who gave up, grew apathetic, and retreated from fellow prisoners often died. A formal, detailed study of patients admitted to a general hospital revealed that many of them had experienced a prolonged period of feeling either hopeless or helpless in the months preceding the symptoms of their illnesses.[*] This appeared to be a form of giving up in response to change, stress, or loss in their lives.

These brief examples only illustrate the type of thinking being done by some scientists attempting to understand better the role of life circumstances in the development of physical illness. Current evidence suggests that life circumstances can play either a predisposing or precipitating role in the physical illness of many individuals. Such life circumstances may be neither necessary nor sufficient for the development of a particular individual's illness—but the clues suggest that we are achieving a better understanding of the ways in which

---

[*] Engel, G. L. A. A psychological setting of somatic disease: The 'giving-up, given-up' complex. *Proceedings of the Royal Society of Medicine,* 60:533, 1967.

life circumstances may increase the susceptibility of many persons to a wide variety of illnesses.

THE FAMILY AND ILLNESS

There are several ways in which what goes on in the family may influence family members' susceptibility to illness. The internal stress that is a part of daily life in troubled families may make family members more vulnerable to all illnesses. Here, one would expect the family to have a large number of illnesses which would occur at all times. One would not expect clustering of illness. All or most family members would experience the illness, although the fact that different members of a family may be more or less attached or connected to the family could influence how equally the high rate of illness was shared.

A second pattern might involve the clustering of family illnesses in a period following many life changes, stress, or loss. During most of the time, the number of illnesses would not be unusual, but the family's response to the death of a loved one, for example, would not be effective in coping with the stress and all or most family members would be vulnerable to all illnesses for a period of time.

A third way in which what goes on in the family could influence the illnesses of family members does not concern the susceptibility to illness, but how long illnesses last. Internal tension within the family could delay recovery from illness. The pattern here would be a tendency for family members' illnesses to last much longer than they do in other persons. Put another way, this could be called a family tendency towards chronic illnesses.

As with the studies of individual life circumstances, there is some evidence to support each of these three patterns in families. Families with high illness rates over extended periods of time have been recognized. In a study of 100 families over ten years, for example, it was found that some families demonstrated very low rates of illness for the ten-year period and others very high rates.* The study was not designed to lead to understanding of family conflict or other

---

* Dingle, J. H., Badger, G. F., and Jordan, W. S.. Jr, *Illness in the Home: A Study of 25,000 Illnesses in a Group of Cleveland Families.* The Press of Western Reserve University, Cleveland, 1964.

sources of family tension, but the investigators concluded that there may be a way of being a family that is associated with a great deal of physical illness. Over a shorter period of time, our own research demonstrated great differences among families in the amount of illness. It appears that there is some evidence to suggest that some families have high rates of physical illness over time.

The second pattern of clusters of family illnesses has been demonstrated also. Some families go for many months with only a few minor upper-respiratory or gastrointestinal illnesses and then experience a period of several months in which different family members have a wide variety of apparently unrelated illnesses.* What has not been demonstrated clearly, however, is the relationship of clusters of family illnesses to life stress. Although observations of family life in a natural, rather than research, setting provide less conclusive evidence, there are families who appear to respond to the separation or loss of a family member with increased susceptibility to illness.

The third pattern—family tension sustaining illness with a resulting tendency towards chronic illness—has been noted for over 30 years.* Astute physicians have observed that either chronic illness or repeated episodes of acute illness may well have something to do with the family of the patient. Other clinicians have speculated that the rewards of illness for some patients include family attention, consideration, and "specialness." These secondary effects of being sick may prolong the illness in some families.

These research clues suggest the possibility of learning something about preventing some of the illness family members experience. At the present time, however, the recognition of one of the three patterns—high family illness rates over time, family illness following change, stress, or loss, and a tendency to chronic illness in the family —should serve as a signal to take a look at the family and search for sources of stress that may be changed.

FAMILY ADJUSTMENT TO ILLNESS

Although, for some families and some illnesses, what goes on in the family may influence suceptibility, all families must, at times,

---

* Kellner, R. *Family Ill Health.* C. C Thomas, Springfield, Ill., 1963.
* Richardson, H. B. *Patients Have Families.* Commonwealth Fund, New York, 1945.

cope with illness in a family member. Regardless of whether family factors are one of the causes, each family must make some type of adjustment to the illness. The factors that influence the nature of the family adjustment are many:

1) the overall competence of the family
2) the family role of the sick member
3) the seriousness of the illness
4) the presence of others to offer the family support
5) the sick individual's response to the illness.

The competence of the family—their strengths and assets as a group—plays an important part in the family's response. Healthy families, with their shared power, high levels of individuality and closeness, excellent problem-solving ability, and openness to feelings, are in an ideal position to deal with a family member's illness. As pointed out in discussing family stress (Chapter XII), if the stress is severe and its duration long, even the healthiest of families will begin to move from a fairly flexible organization to one that is much more rigid and, if the situation goes on, to a more chaotic structure. Troubled families are much more likely to show some evidence of distintegration in their function—a movement towards a chaotic organization. The difference between a healthy family's response to a severe illness and that of a troubled family can be seen in the following vignettes.

At 42, Jack Howard experienced a severe head injury in an automobile accident. He was in a coma and cared for in the intensive care unit of the hospital. For several weeks, it was not known if he would live or die, and when it became apparent he was going to live, there were several months of uncertainty about how disabled he would be.

Jack and Mary Howard and their two teen-aged sons were a close family. Both Jack and Mary were capable of making family decisions; each was a competent person, and together they provided the family with strong leadership. Their sons were accustomed to participating in family decisions. The family shared feelings, whether anger fear, joy, sadness, or disappointment.

After the immediate shock of Jack's accident, Mary and the

boys spent a good deal of time talking in the intensive care waiting room. Two aspects of their talk seemed particularly important. First, they were able to express their individual fears, uncertainties, sadness, and other feelings about Jack's critical condition. Second, as a group they planned together how to manage the day-to-day details of life. Eating, sleeping, the boys' school, care of their home, and other daily concerns were discussed and a plan of action agreed upon. They had much help available to them from relatives, friends, and neighbors, and they were able to accept these offers and yet remain a cohesive family group. Although each had private concerns and anxieties, for the most part they were together and could share the pain of this frightening experience. No one felt alone.

Ted Hall was 44 when he suffered a massive heart attack. He was in the coronary care unit of the hospital for nine days, before being transferred to a private room. During the first week, there was considerable uncertainty about whether Ted would survive, and later, when his survival seemed assured, there were a great many questions about how severely he would be disabled.

Ted and Ellen Hall and their three children were a family strongly dominated by Ted's authoritarian approach to life. He believed that every situation could be handled by relying on a series of firm rules—and the Hall family's rules were Ted's. He ran the family as if it were a military unit in which all the orders came from the top. Ellen had found this tight, rigid organization stifling, but the lack of responsibility had been acceptable to her in many ways. The children were not accustomed to acting independently or with much initiative. The older son was rebellious and often in trouble at school. The family had accepted that Ted would make all decisions and that he was not accustomed to sharing that responsibility. Ted's rules also prohibited the open expression of feelings—particularly feelings of fear, sadness, or anger.

The Hall family quickly fell apart after receiving the news of Ted's heart attack and critical condition. They seemed to have no idea of what to do. Ellen, for example, had not been permitted to write checks, did not know the family's economic condition, and only had $20 in her purse from her weekly food allowance. The two younger children seemed frightened, and each sat quietly in the waiting room. The older boy wandered off to "have a beer" with some friends. Neither Ellen nor the older boy seemed able to provide leadership. There was no sharing of feelings, and each member felt very much alone. There was no discussion about how to manage the details of daily life. The family seemed to drift aimlessly from hour to hour. This disorganized and chaotic state was relieved on the fourth day by the arrival of Ellen's parents. Her father took over immediately and used his considerable authority to reorganize the family.

Although both the Howards and the Halls were facing the serious stress of the possible loss of the father, the responses of the families were very different. The Howards, a healthy family, had the strengths and skills to deal with this threat. They were prepared to share both their feelings and the responsibility for daily life. The Halls, a troubled family of the dominated type, were totally unprepared to deal with the stress of Ted's serious illness. They did not have the strengths and skills and rapidly moved to a chaotic structure until rescued by another authoritarian figure, Ellen's father.

The family role of the sick member is another important factor that influences the family's response to illness. Healthy families tend to deal with any member's illness more effectively, but even with such families the threat of loss of either parent may pose additional stress. The Hall family represents the particular stress a dominated family faces when illness strikes the dominant member. In some families, a member is particularly valued for certain individual characteristics .A child with outstanding academic, athletic, or artistic skill may play a special family role in which much of what is considered "good" about the family is deposited in the child's future. Illness in that child, particularly if it threatens the child's life or restricts his or her potential, may pose an unusual problem for the family. In a somewhat related way, some families "dump" everything bad or negative about the family on one child. If this scapegoated child becomes ill, the family's guilt may interfere with their capacity to cope effectively. Even if the sick child has not been the family scapegoat, the course of the illness and the family's response to it may lead to guilt.

As a young intern, I was the staff member assigned to a young man dying of chronic kidney disease. This was in the early days of the artificial kidney, but even that came to be of little help. During his final hospitalization, he became difficult to manage. He whined and cried a lot and placed great demands on his parents and sisters to "do something." Perhaps in part out of identification with a person my own age, I made unusual attempts to be helpful, spending a great deal of time with him and searching broadly for medications with which to ease his pain. The family became increasingly irritated with his demands and, at the same time, very grateful for my attempts to help. I noted that they visited him less and less as the weeks went on and his death approached.

On the night of his death, I called the family and suggested they come to the hospital. An hour later they had not arrived, and he died quietly. Wishing to inform them personally, I called again and told them the end was at hand and to come at once. An hour later they had not come and my next call found them still at home. I felt I had no choice but to tell them that their son had died. The following telephone conversation ensued:

Me: "I hate to tell you—but Jim has passed away."
Father: "You son-of-a-bitch."
Me: "I beg your par . . ."
Father: "You killed him—you dirty bastard."
Me: "What do you . . ."
Mother: (screaming into the phone) "You killed my baby—you killed my baby."

This conversation went on for a minute or so longer with the intensity of their rage at me increasing with each statement. Badly shaken, I hung up and remained distressed until the following day when the psychiatrist consulting on the ward could help me understand the intolerable guilt the family experienced and projected onto me.

This family's emotional resources had been exhausted by their son's long illness and dying. Although they could not face openly their wish for his inevitable death to come quickly, that underlying shared wish led to massive guilt. When their wish was fulfilled they went through a brief period of blaming someone else (me) for the death they wished for.

The seriousness of the family member's illness is, of course, a factor in determining the family's capacity to cope effectively with the illness. The more serious and life-threatening the illness, the greater the stress on most families. Another major source of stress to the family's adaptive capacity is the degree of uncertainty in the outcome of the illness. Not knowing what may happen to a family member can be almost as stressful for some families as facing the loss of that member.

Chronic illness may be particularly difficult for many families to cope with. The family may need to reorganize itself on a more-or-less permanent basis, which is often more difficult than dealing with acute, but time-limited, stressful illness.

The support of others can play a crucial role in a family's ability to cope with illness. Relatives and friends may play an important role and temporarily take over some of the family's usual responsibilities. However, there is a need to fit the help to the needs of the family. The authoritarian help that Ellen's father gave the Hall family was appropriate to the chaotic condition of that family. If, however, the same kind of help had been thrust upon the Howard family, it might have gotten in the way of that family's effective coping and actually been experienced by the family as an additional and unwelcome stress. People who wish to help must sense what kind of help is actually needed for each family.

A final factor influencing the family's capacity to cope effectively with a family member's illness is how the family member is dealing with the illness. There are two parts of an individual's response to an illness. The first involves the individual's specific personality characteristics, fears, hope, strengths, and vulnerabilities. Those individuals who can be reasonably open with others about their concerns and fears and who can allow others to take over for them and take care of them make it easier for most families to cope. Those individuals who refuse to acknowledge their illnesses, the gravity of their situations, or the need for others to take over pose additional stress for the family. Individuals who quickly give in totally to the illness and become childlike in their reactions also represent unusual stress for family members.

In addition to these more-or-less specific aspects of an individual's response to illness, there are reactions that occur in most people when they are ill. To one degree or another, there are numerous consequences of being ill, and the extent to which the family is aware of and deals with them may influence the capacity of the family to cope and to be helpful to the sick member. These general reactions include a loss of the individual's sense of invulnerability—the "how can this be happening to me" feeling. Sick persons often feel a real loss of control over their lives and an increasing sense of disconnection from their usual network of friends and acquaintances. Finally, many sick persons demonstrate some impairment in their thinking which is restricted to their thoughts about the illness itself. Patients often can discuss business or politics with great clarity, but may think in a very distorted and emotional way about their illness. For example intelligent, educated individuals may often feel that their illness has been brought about as a punishment for thoughts or deeds or as a result of ill feelings others have had for them.

It can be seen that the family is very much involved with illness. The available evidence suggests that what goes on in the family may influence the susceptibility of family members to illness. Once illness develops in a family member, the family must cope with it as best they can. Some do this with great effectiveness, while other families disintegrate. Some of the factors that influence the amount of stress the illness poses for the family have been described. In sum, it is difficult to escape the conclusion that the family may be involved in every aspect of illness.

XIV

Change and Loss

The ability of the family to deal with change and loss is a real test of its competence. When one looks at a family in a state of stress, it is often assumed that, in the past, the family had a stable environment. It is probably more accurate to assume that the world has always been changing and presenting new challenges, uncertainties, and fears to the family. Led by an explosive technology, the world is indeed a difficult place in which the family must survive. In fact, some write that the family is dead or dying—that divorce, single-parent families, and the growing number of combined families are the symptoms of the family's terminal phase. Others point to the large number of single persons—widowed, divorced, or never married—now living in our society without the support of the extended family. To each dire pronouncement there are a number of interpretations.

It is clear that, in the big, rapid, and uncertain world, changes pose particular difficulties. Some changes—for example, the combination of inflation and high unemployment, the declining value of our currency, the intricacies of international agreements—are hard to understand; further, it is difficult for an individual or family to exert any influence on the outcome of such changes. This impotence, combined with difficulty in understanding the problems and uncertainty about what the real problems are, makes for alarm about future change and a longing for presumably simpler times. Worldwide and national changes provide the backdrop for changes that occur closer to home.

157

The cities, towns, and neighborhoods in which families live may change, either toward deterioration and chaos or toward order and improvement. Sizes change and neighborhoods become crowded, or people leave and empty dwellings become prominent. These changes add to the circumstances with which each family must contend.

In addition to external changes, there are inevitable, natural alterations occurring over time in the family itself: Children grow up and parents age. These two processes of maturation and aging can be thought of as occurring in stages. Each stage presents specific problems and developmental tasks that the family must meet and solve. The overlapping stages offer a convenient mechanism for thinking about the family over time. The stages to be described are:

1) early marriage
2) parenthood
3) young children
4) adolescent chlidren
5) children as young adults
6) empty nest
7) growing old

EARLY MARRIAGE

In Chapter II, some of the factors involved in bringing a particular couple together in marriage were described. The early period of that marriage—whether it be a year or longer—entails two basic tasks. The first is for the spouses to complete separation from their parents and gradually evolve a relationship in which each spouse experiences the other as the most important person in his or her life. The second task is to establish the basic rules of their relationship.

By the time they marry, many persons have separated emotionally from their parents and families and are leading autonomous lives. Others, however, are still firmly attached and must transfer these bonds to their spouses. This does not mean that individuals stop loving their parents and other family members, but that their spouses become the basic source to which they look for gratification of personal needs like love, support, and companionship. This is a complicated process, frequently taking several years to accomplish. If an individual has grown up in a family in which individuality and autonomy were encouraged, the task is easier. Growing up in a family in which great dependency on the family was encouraged can interfere. Parents can make this transition a difficult one. ("No matter whom you marry, you'll always be my baby.") Newly married couples can be attached to both families of origin, creating fierce competition over the issue of family loyalty. Some families with grown children, for example, have never had a Christmas in their own home, but "go to grandma's" or alternate rigidly from one spouse's parental home to the other. Often, one spouse in particular has difficulty with this emotional separation, and it becomes a source of serious marital conflict. Occasionally, his or her most important relationship is with parents rather than spouse. The spouse either battles this or gives in and becomes an appendage to the in-law family.

> Jodie Brown was still closely attached to her family after four childless years of marriage to Arnold. She visited with her mother every morning, called her every night to say "good night," insisted that she and Arnold have dinner at her parents' home every Sunday, and planned each summer vacation with her parents. If Jodie had decisions to make or problems to solve, she turned to her mother. She and her mother talked about her relationship with Arnold, but she refused to discuss her relationship with her mother with Arnold.
>
> Arnold resented these conditions, and after a long period of trying to change them, went along with them in a quiet, sullen manner. Increasingly, he sought the companionship of male friends to go to ball games, hunting, and to visit and drink beer. Jodie, in turn, complained bitterly of Arnold's "rejection" of her.

Most couples have already made a solid start on the construction of the rules of their relationship by the time they marry. They hardly ever sit down and draw up rules; rather, they tend to evolve them. Both come to the marriage carrying not only personality traits which will either mesh or conflict with those of the spouses, but also a model of their parents' relationships. Under optimal circumstances, each partner has personality characteristics that complement those of the spouse and carries a model of a parental relationship that was close and effective. These conditions prepare them for a smooth and reasonably conflict-free early stage of being a family. However, when the spouses have very different models of what their relationship should be, they need to gradually evolve a set of stable and mutually acceptable rules.

The rules themselves must define a way of dealing with power: who has the right to decide what, how differences of opinion will be settled, who is to play what role with certain types of problems.

The rules must also govern the inevitable trade-offs that a relationship involves—that is, what each individual is willing to give up in order to get something. Many couples develop a more-or-less stable pattern of exchange during the early years of their relationship.

Rules are also evolved about the levels of communication the relationship will tolerate. In some marriages, only events are reported or small talk allowed. In other relationships, sharing ideas is encouraged. In others, everyday feelings and private thoughts are permissible. In some marriages, deeply personal feelings and thoughts are exchanged. Early in the relationship, the couple begins to work out the rules that govern what levels of communication will occur and under what circumstances each level will be encouraged or permitted.

The couple must also evolve rules about closeness and distance in their relationship. Under what conditions is what degree of closeness allowed? What are the circumstances under which it is permissible for there to be greater distance in the relationship and privacy for the individuals?

There are many more mutually acceptable patterns each couple evolves, such as those having to do with sex, relationships with each individual's parents, involvement with friends, individual and shared activities, and responsibility for money, household duties, and paying bills.

Ed and Connie Stanton had a very difficult first year of marriage and sought professional help when it appeared that they were moving towards a divorce. Although Connie was a strong, forceful woman and Ed a gentle and less aggressive man, neither of them had significant individual emotional problems. Rather, they had not been able to make a start in working out the rules of their relationship.

Connie, a successful account executive in an advertising

agency, was providing all of their income while Ed was in his final year of law school. She felt, as a consequence, that she should handle all the money. Ed disagreed with this, but was less than direct about it because of his discomfort about being supported by his wife. He felt that they should agree on each financial decision, but had no clear ideas about what should be done to solve disagreements. Both Connie and Ed were unaccustomed to negotiation, and each grew angrier as the other insisted on his or her own way.

Connie was most comfortable talking about ideas and avoided sharing deep feelings. Ed came from a family in which there was a great deal of sharing of feelings, and was frustrated when his attempts to share with Connie were evaded. Ed and Connie were also unable to work out any agreeable pattern for their sexual relationship. Ed felt that they should make love when either of them desired it, while Connie felt either should have the right of refusal.

This young couple was failing to find a way of living together that was satisfactory to both individuals. Rules about power, sex, trade-offs, and communication did not evolve, and the relationship was heading for trouble.

The early phase of the marriage is like infancy in that life long patterns of behavior are being established. In many ways, the relationship is still in its formative period, and adaptation is easier than after years of unresolved differences.

PARENTHOOD

Under the best of circumstances, the couple has accomplished the two basic tasks of the stage of early marriage before having their first child. If they have not and are still struggling with separation from their own families and evolving mutually satisfactory relationship rules, having a baby may increase the conflict and turmoil within the marital relationship.

There are several issues the couple must face during this period of great change:

1) To whom does the baby belong?
2) How is the mothering to be shared?
3) Is the marital relationship going to remain the parents' most important relationship?

The birth of the infant and the development of the strong, necessary, and natural mother-infant bond present a problem to the
couple. When the mother feels and behaves in a way that communicates to her husband that the baby is "hers" and not "theirs,"
the husband is effectively excluded from the relationship. She may
not wish this, and the impetus may come from the husband who, for
example, is uncomfortable with the part of him that is nourishing
and often identified as feminine. Regardless of how it starts, the
unspoken agreement that the baby is the wife's rather than theirs can
be the start of serious trouble for the couple. When, despite the
natural intensity of the mother-infant bond, the baby is not solely
the mother's, there is a much greater likelihood that the husband will
not feel totally excluded nor the wife totally responsible.

This issue may be reflected in the extent to which the husband
participates in the care: How often does he feed, change or bathe
the infant? Does he share the getting up at night? Is there a rigid
assignment of responsibility—"I'll make the money and you take care
of the baby?" The inclusion of the husband in the parenting does not
blur the special nature of the mother-infant relationship. Even when
the exclusion of the father is acceptable to both parents and does not
lead to marital conflict, the parents may miss an opportunity for a
special type of sharing.

Although much of the couple's life necessarily centers about the
care of the new baby, this is the period in which a pattern is being
established. If there is significant sharing of the care, the couple
experiences this as a new and gratifying part of their relationship. If,
however, the husband is left out or excludes himself and does not
participate, the couple have not shared this exciting experience. The
issue of how important the couple's relationship is to be, how much
time and attention are to be devoted to it, is crucial. Preferably there
is a balance in which the couple takes the time to insure the continued growth of their relationship. Both parents can receive im-
mense satisfaction from the infant and their parenting, but if this is not
shared and if they do not make opportunities to be alone together,
their relationship will suffer.

When Holly was born, Mark and Karen Lester were delighted. From the start, Mark was very much involved with

Holly's care. Although an intern and very busy, he found great satisfaction in holding his daughter. He gave her the evening bottle, changed her diapers, bathed her, and often got up at night to change, rock, and feed her. For Karen and Mark, the baby was "theirs" and, when possible, Mark did some of the mothering. Karen experienced great satisfaction in her relationship with Holly, but was relieved to have Mark's practical assistance and delighted in the sense of sharing. From shortly after Holly's birth, however, Mark and Karen continued their practice of going out one night each week and, although initially there was some concern about leaving Holly with a sitter, they soon came to be comfortable about it. They arranged Holly's care (as much as possible) so that the late evenings, when Mark was home and not on duty, included some time for them to talk, watch TV, listen to their record collection, and just "be together."

YOUNG CHILDREN

This stage of the family is often complicated by the fact that many couples have a new infant when their firstborn becomes mobile and needs to explore the yard, new little friends, the nursery school, and ultimately elementary school. Life becomes much more involved for the parents. There are so many needs to be met and often so little time in which to meet them all. Young children need a good deal of supervision and protection, but at the same time they need encouragement to be more independent. These needs are just part of the total scene. Mother has her needs, Father has his own, and, if a new infant is present, his or her needs are urgent. Separate from each individual's needs, the parental couple has needs in order to continue the growth of their relationship. Some type of system must evolve that offers both the couple and each family member some satisfaction. Under most circumstances, they evolve some clear division of responsibility. This can require the husband to care for some of the children's needs. He may feed the infant, play with the young children, and bathe or put to bed one or all of them. It is when the husband does not share this responsibility or is excluded from it by the wife that the wife's level of fatigue is such that, even if she wants to have time and energy for the marital relationship, she is too tired to talk, make love, see a movie, visit friends, or in any way do those things which help the continued growth of the parents' relationship. This stage of family life may deteriorate into stress and conflict.

ADOLESCENT CHILDREN

As the children enter adolescence, new skills are required of the family. These involve the need of the parents to provide encouragement and support, clear structure and guidelines, and the freedom for their adolescent children to do some experimenting on their own. By this time, the couple has often established the basic pattern of their relationship and the tone and tempo of family life. If the family is a flexible one, the period of so-called "adolescent turmoil" can proceed with considerable smoothness. Family life need not be stormy just because one or more children are in adolescence. There is, however, always parental concern. As children are more on their own—making more decisions independently, driving automobiles or riding motorcycles, competing for school offices, engaging in athletics, being exposed to drugs and kids who use them—the parents have real and increasing concern.

When the children are in adolescence, one sees whether the parental style is "control the kid" or "help the kid grow." Anxiety makes some parents mostly controllers—they strive to control their children and their life circumstances. When adolescence is reached, the likelihood of parental success with continuing control is diminished. Open or subtle revolt against stringent parental controls is too easy for many adolescents to achieve. During this period, children need to be encouraged, whenever appropriate, to make their own decisions. If the pattern of family life has involved shared power, encouragement of individuality, negotiating differences, clear communication, and openness to feelings, the family's adaptation to having adolescent children can be calm and harmonious. But, if the family has been dominated by one powerful parent or has been severely conflicted, problems are likely to increase when the children become distant and rebellious.

At this time, either the parents' relationship will deepen or conflict will increase. Often, smoldering, undercover conflicts break into the open. Most often these have to do with power. Who has the right to decide whether Janie can date at 14, Tom have the car at 16, or Mary go to a weekend party at the university when she is 17 and a high school senior?

Sam and Helen Grant had always fought a lot. They seldom agreed and, in particular, had never come to any sort of agreement about power. As long as their two sons were little, however, the intensity of Sam and Helen's underlying disagreement and periods of open conflict had been moderate. As the boys became adolescents, the frequency and intensity of the parental conflict increased. If Sam thought their older son should have the car for a date, Helen didn't. If Helen felt that one of the boys should be allowed to do something, Sam opposed it. They were rarely together on any issue and, as a result, both boys found ways to do things secretly or to find the support of one parent to do something that would be kept from the other parent. Life in the Grant family became increasingly stormy, and Sam and Helen told their friends that having adolescents was "hell."

CHILDREN AS YOUNG ADULTS

This period of family life involves the increasing separation of the children and the preparation of the parents for that time when the children have become independent. The parents must face that soon, on a day-to-day basis, they will have only each other. Letting go of the young adult children may be hampered by underlying parental concerns that what they have going with each other will not be enough. Other couples, however, who, throughout earlier stages of family development, have maintained the central importance of their relationship, may look forward to the children's separation with pleasure. The freedom it allows the couple—the additional time for each other, simple discoveries like how easy it is to cook for two, having a house or apartment entirely to themselves, time for new ventures, and pride in competent offspring—can effectively compensate for the bittersweet regret that time passes so quickly and leads to the breaking up of "the old gang."

Under the best of circumstances, the parents' relationship has continued to change and grow. They understand each other and can read each other well. Each has become more tolerant of the other's mistakes and idiosyncracies. They have worked out a stable and mutually satisfying set of rules for their relationship. They feel very much together and offer much support to each other. They have found it increasingly easier to share deep feelings and thoughts. The future, without the children, looks good.

For those less fortunate couples who have less satisfactory relationships, there may be a good deal of underlying fear. The conflict or emptiness of their relationship offers little hope for the future. This is the marital setting in which one or both may enter a "mid-life crisis." The form such a crisis can take varies from person to person. It may be depression or, conversely, plunging into frantic activities. It may take the form of an extramarital affair, a precipitous job change, or the sudden adoption of a new, "mod" life-style. The form of the crisis is determined mostly by the individual's personality, but whether or not one occurs is clearly related to the nature of the marital relationship.

Bea and Hank Smith had a distant type of relationship. Hank tended to quietly dominate Bea and she, in turn, was unhappy and mildly hypochondriacal. She felt shut out of his life, and he resented her nagging. The strength of their relationship had been their shared involvement with their two daughters. They never missed any of the girls' school or social activities, but had little life of their own. Both daughters finished college, and each was engaged to be married. Hank began to feel depressed, considered leaving the company he had been with for 25 years, and had his first extramarital affair with a young woman at his office. Bea began a series of almost frantic activities. She started a crash diet, joined an exercise class, and began taking yoga lessons. Every moment of each day was scheduled, and it appeared that, most of all, she wished to avoid contemplation.

EMPTY NEST

When the children have left and are settled into lives of their own, the parents experience what they have been anticipating for several years. There are often happy surprises for those couples who feared this period of being alone again. I have been impressed that some relationships do not truly blossom until the children have gone. What had appeared to be a troubled marriage centered around the children and their activities became a much closer and more satisfying relationship.

Tod and Joan Hinkle seemed to have everything necessary for happiness. Tod had achieved outstanding success and Joan was a leader in their community. Both of their children had done well in school and with their friends. Yet, Tod and Joan's relationship had always contained a sour core. Joan did not feel that Tod was affectionate, and she often resented the time he spent with his business. Tod felt that Joan's demands were excessive, that he could never please her, and that he got little in return.

Their two children seemed to bind them together, but close friends were concerned that when both of the children had left, Tod and Joan's relationship would fall apart. Contrary to this, the relationship improved dramatically. Both Tod and Joan turned to each other. He began taking a good deal of time off from his business, and they spent it together. They talked more, and both felt they were getting a much greater part of the other. Joan stopped spending most of her time in community activities and, as a couple, they entertained less. They were more comfortable with each other, shared more of their deeper feelings, and their sexual relationship became satisfactory to both. Their friends commented that they were more fun to be with as a couple—the sourness was gone.

Sometimes it is difficult to understand this kind of late blossoming of a relationship. At a very general level, their shared interest in their children probably saved their marriage from dissolving and, at the same time, prevented it from growing. With the children gone, it was going to either fall apart or grow. Fortunately, for many couples growth does occur and the relationship is better than it ever had been.

GROWING OLD

Unfortunately for many, growing old is a time of loneliness, sadness, and bitterness. Everyone's body ages, but the culture seems to value only youth. If the older person is single, the problems are often multiplied. Since the inflationary economy impacts most severely on the aged with fixed incomes, the quality of life often deteriorates. This picture of aging is true for far too many persons; however, it is not true for all. The most important defense against the kind of massive pain pictured above is the continuation of a close and good relationship with husband or wife.

The marital relationship, although basically stable, must continue to change. Aging occurs at different rates for husband and wife, and this often requires either subtle or drastic changes in the relationship.

A wife, for example, may have lived comfortably with a strong and somewhat dominant husband. If he ages more rapidly, they may struggle to work out a new relationship in which she gradually assumes more power or influence in their relationship than ever before. She must be willing to do this, and he must be willing or acquiesce to this change. For an aging couple who have shared power equally, the transition will be smooth if more rapid aging of one requires the other gradually to assume more of the responsibility for day-to-day living. These issues may precipitate some conflict, but often are handled without conflict.

> Paul and Ruth Suttle had experienced a strong, close relationship throughout the 45 years of their marriage. Their three children had families of their own, lived in distant cities, and were doing well. Ruth, at 70, presented greater evidence of aging than Paul, who was 75. Her memory was faulty and physically she was not as well preserved. She insisted, however, on continuing to do the grocery shopping, cooking, and paying the household bills. As this became more and more difficult for her, Paul just quietly moved into a helping position. He did not try to take over Ruth's responsibilities, but to share them. They gradually came to shop, cook, and write the monthly checks together. It was a gradual and subtle change, and was accomplished without either conflict or loss of self-respect for Ruth.

Under the best of circumstances, the couple may continue to be independent and autonomous. Often, the nature of their relationship with their grown children may change, with the aging couple looking more to their children for support, advice, and assistance.

The evidence grows that couples can maintain an active sexual life into their eighties or longer. The most frequent cause of an individual's declining sexual activity during old age is the absence of an available and interested partner.

Most of all, however, this last stage of life can be shared with the person who has been there through it all. The mistakes, losses, joys, and "might have beens" are part of the relationship. The communication that plays such an important role in each person's need for a sense of connection to others can continue. The need to reach out and touch another, to sleep with a loved one's arms around you, to complain to someone about the economy or weather—in so many ways the relationship may offer each partner that which makes the older years worthwhile and gives them a measure of joy.

Perhaps the greatest despair of all for the aged is loneliness. The following quote speaks to that with simple eloquence.

> "That man there can't hear nothin'. We got the money together one time to get him a hearin' aid. He wore it for about a week and then just set it aside. He works all day doin' people's yards. Says he don't have to hear out there and everything else he hears makes him nervous. So in the evenings when he comes in he turns on that little TV and just lays there on the couch watchin' pictures. And I set right here at my quiltin'.
>
> "Maybe that don't sound like much, but it's not lonesome. I was real lonesome once after my first husband died and I don't want no more of that.
>
> "And he cooks supper ever other night. Gives me more time to be at my work. And I'm grateful for the cookin'.
>
> "He ain't lonesome either."*

In this brief review of the stages of family life, the emphasis has been on the need for and capacity of the family to deal with ever-present change. Those couples and families who work out satisfactory early relationships are most likely to have the flexibility to deal with these internal changes as well as those ongoing changes in neighborhood, town, city, and world.

LOSS

Many of the changes to which the family must adapt involve loss. A couple loses something of their privacy and time for each other by having children. As children grow, the couple loses having little ones. As children leave, the parents lose an important part of their life together. Parents lose their youth, their sense of physical indestructibility, their productive years at work and, ultimately, all but a sliver of their future. Loss, and the family's ability to deal with it, are, therefore, central to dealing with change.

---

* Cooper, Patricia, and Buferd, Norma Bradly. *The Quilters: Women and Domestic Art*. Doubleday and Co., Garden City, New York, 1977.

At its most painful intensity, loss involves the death of loved ones. In many ways, this is the ultimate test of the family's strength. Can the loss be accepted? Can the family mourn? Can the family pick up the pieces and get on with life? Perhaps the single most important family characteristic which influences the family's capacity to deal with loss is the ability to be open with feelings. The feelings of shock, anger, and profound sadness that follow the death of a loved one will be experienced by all. The question is: Will they be felt only alone or will there be some sharing? Those families who can share openly such painful feelings encourage a sense of being together which offers some easing of the painful wound. For those who do not have this type of openness, each family member's pain must be experienced alone, and this adds to the burden.

In many families, a time of grief is a period in which the family's religious beliefs and practices offer great help. They may offer an understanding of the meaning of life and the role of death as well as provide the framework for the necessary celebration of the deceased person's significance to the survivors.

Whether a family is religious or not, the death of a loved one brings the family's basic values into clear focus. What is life about? What is the meaning of our existence with each other? For many, the realization emerges that fame and fortune are, ultimately, weak substitutes for the meaning to be found within the family.

XV

How's Your Family?

Now that we have looked at families at various points on the continuum of family functioning, let us return to the questionnaires which were presented at the beginning of the volume. This will give readers an opportunity to evaluate their families and to compare their answers with those of healthy families.

The questions and the answers are, of course, based on our research with both healthy and troubled families. It is important to re-emphasize that, with few exceptions, the families were white, of middle and upper-middle socio-economic classes, and intact. Each family studied could be placed at a point on a continuum of families which ranged from healthy to severely troubled. The continuum itself is based on the extent to which a family accomplishes the two major tasks of the family: the stabilization of the parents' personalities (or encouraging their continued development), and the production of autonomous children. Healthy families do these two jobs very well; severely troubled families do neither well; all other families fall between these two extremes.

Although many readers will have recognized their families from the descriptions of healthy, faltering, troubled, or severely troubled families, others may have some questions, and this chapter is a further effort to help identify where a family may be on the continuum of family competence.

Before proceeding to the questionnaires themselves, however, a few words are necessary about the way they were constructed and how they can be used. The questions were taken from the facts presented in each of the chapters. They were not presented to the families studied, but rather are based upon what was learned from the families. This resulted in questions which I answered as if I were a member of a 1) healthy, 2) faltering, 3) troubled, or 4) severely troubled family. These answers form the scoring key for the two questionnaires. In effect, when readers answer the questions regarding the whole family, they obtain information regarding whether their family is healthy or faltering as contrasted to troubled or severely troubled. To facilitate scoring, the answer expected of a healthy or faltering family has been marked with an "X". If the answers suggest that one's family is either healthy or faltering, one can obtain information useful in distinguishing these two levels of family functioning from the parental relationship questionnaire.

These questions were selected because of the high likelihood that members of both healthy and faltering families would answer them alike and that members of troubled and severely troubled families would answer them differently. It is to be emphasized that it is not expected that members of every healthy or faltering family will answer each question the way I believe they would be answered, but that most of the questions produce answers as indicated.

If you recognized your family from the descriptions in earlier chapters as either healthy or faltering and answered most of the 25 questions as members of either healthy or faltering families would, you have a good idea that your family is one of those two types. This suggestion is strengthened if there were only a few questions for which individual family members gave very different answers—for example, "Applies a Lot" and "Does Not Apply at All."

If questions remain as to whether your family is healthy or faltering, it may be helpful to examine the parents' responses to the parental relationship questionnaire. The same instructions apply for this questionnaire. "H" indicates the answer for healthy families; "F" indicates the answer for faltering families.

WHOLE FAMILY QUESTIONNAIRE

IN OUR FAMILY:	Does not apply at all	Applies a little	Applies a lot	Impossible to answer, don't know
1. Both parents are the leaders. Neither is always dominant.			X	
2. We can trust other family members not to hurt our feelings deliberately.			X	
3. We believe that outsiders will often take advantage of us.	X			
4. Relatives and friends usually take over when we're having trouble.	X			
5. The children are encouraged to try new things.			X	
6. We fight a lot.	X			
7. Someone often acts as if he or she knows what I am thinking or feeling.	X			
8. We often avoid facing problems until the last minute.	X			
9. It is OK to express sadness.			X	
10. Stress often leads to everyone going separate ways.	X			
11. We are good at solving problems.			X	
12. We don't have to feel ashamed of feelings.			X	
13. We almost always talk about superficial things.	X			
14. I can really be an individual.			X	
15. We are supposed to let people know what our ideas are.			X	
16. It is OK to express joy or happiness.			X	
17. Our feelings don't get ridiculed or put down.			X	
18. It is OK to have our own thoughts and ideas.			X	
19. We are often angry.	X			
20. We are encouraged to start new things.			X	
21. Stress often results in one family member making all the decisions.	X			
22. People let me know they've heard what I think and feel.			X	
23. We are often sad or depressed.	X			
24. It is OK to be interested in things that don't interest anyone else.			X	
25. We often feel "what's the use?"	X			

PARENTAL RELATIONSHIP QUESTIONNAIRE

IN OUR FAMILY:	Does not apply at all	Applies a little	Applies a lot	Impossible to answer, don't know
1. My wife (husband) and I can talk about our deep feelings and very private thoughts.	F		H	
2. I feel hopeless about ever getting what I need and want emotionally from my wife (husband).	H		F	
3. I find my wife (husband) physically attractive.	F		H	
4. My relationship with one of my parents or a friend is very special and, in some ways, closer than my relationship with my wife (husband)	H		F	
5. Sex with my wife (husband) is sometimes a very intimate, "together" experience.	F		H	
6. My personality and that of my wife (husband) seem to fit well together.	F		H	
7. My wife (husband) and I blame each other a lot.	H		F	
8. There is often tension in my relationship with my wife (husband).	H		F	
9. My relationship with one of our children is very special and, in some ways, closer than my relationship with my wife (husband).	H		F	
10. Sex with my wife (husband) is never really satisfactory.	H		F	
11. There is a strong "charge" or good feeling of excitement in my wife's (husband's) and my relationship.	F		H	
12. My wife (husband) and I are best friends.	F		H	
13. The most important part of my relationship with my wife (husband) is our children.	H		F	
14. I am often angry with my wife husband).	H		F	
15. Usually, my wife (husband) and I are openly affectionate with each other.	F		H	
16. Sex with my wife (husband) is sometimes a very fun experience.	F		H	
17. I know my wife (husband) cares deeply for me.	F		H	
18. Sex with my wife (husband) is sometimes a very tender experience.	F		H	
19. My wife (husband) and I have sex about as often as I want to.	F		H	
20. My relationship with my wife (husband) is the closest I've ever had.	F		H	

These 20 questions were selected because of the high likelihood that husbands and wives from healthy families would respond very differently than husbands and wives from faltering families. For each question to which a spouse from a healthy family would respond "Does not apply at all," a spouse from a faltering family would be most apt to respond "Applies a lot." The reverse would also be true; that is, a question most likely to be answered by a spouse from a healthy family with "Applies a lot" would likely be answered "Does not apply at all" by a husband or wife from a faltering family.

Here again, it is not expected that husbands and wives from either healthy or faltering families would answer every question as the score sheet indicates. Rather, it is expected that many questions will be answered in the way indicated and that the exceptions most often will be the use of the response "Applies a little" rather than "Applies a lot" or "Does not apply at all."

It is to be emphasized that these two questionnaires are not intended to be final or definitive indicators. If used, however, to supplement the leads available in the descriptions of the various levels of family competence, they can provide additional information valuable in the assessment of your family.

XVI

What to Do

Most people know whether or not their family is troubled. Life in a troubled family is miserable much of the time. There are often anger and sadness. People in the family either maintain great distance from each other or are constantly nagging and fighting. Rarely is their joy, a feeling of togetherness, or real pleasure in each other's company. Admitting that your family is troubled, however, may involve even more pain. Many families try to avoid or minimize this pain by contrasting themselves favorably to less fortunate families. "At least we don't drink too much like the Smiths," or "We keep our home and yard neat and that's more than you can say about the other families in this neighborhood." These are typical of the statements used to minimize the pain growing out of the open admission that family life is miserable or, at least, not what it might be. Other families protect themselves from painful acknowledgment by comparing themselves favorably to minority groups. "We're not like those damn Blacks, Jews, etc." is typical of this attempt to avoid openly facing the pain and misery within one's own family.

Troubled families often appear in a psychiatrist's office bringing with them the family member who is identified as "the patient." This family member is often disturbed and suffering from a clear-cut psychiatric disturbance. Often the family is obviously troubled with problems and conflicts that may be very different from their complaints and concerns about the patient. Sometimes, however, the patient's disturbance is clearly a reflection of the family problems.

Frequently, the family denies that there is anything wrong with the family. "We're a fine family, doctor, without any problems except there is something wrong with Jimmy," is the type of statement that may protect the family from facing the pain of their shared failure to achieve something close to that which is possible in family life.

Another factor involved in the failure to face the condition of one's family is the simple lack of knowledge of what is possible in family life. Some people grew up in troubled families and then participated in the formation of a second, here-and-now troubled family. The idea that something very different is possible within a family never occurs to them. If you add to this the picture of life in the family as presented on television and in the popular press, it is not hard to understand the disbelief about what is possible in family life.

Although many troubled families deny the existence or extent of their pain and misery, most such families do not. Indeed, in some of our own research we asked family members to rate their families and then compared the ratings to those of experts who had studied the families. There was substantial agreement: Family members privately rated their families much as the experts did.

In particular, healthy families and faltering families rate themselves as the experts do. Often, they ascribe it to luck, but more frequently the parents credit each other. "She (he) is the real reason things go so well in our family. She (he) is a truly remarkable person and it's her (his) love, strength, etc. that is primarily responsible for our family's good fortune." Just as the parents often blame each other for the misery in troubled families, the parents in healthy families frequently give each other the lion's share of the credit.

The greatest denial of family pain is seen often in severely troubled families. Here the intensity of the chaos, hopelessness, and cynicism is such that the reality of what goes on and how bad things really are makes it understandable that family members insist that there is nothing wrong with their family. With the exception, however, of some troubled families and many severely troubled families, most families do a reasonable appraisal of their strengths and liabilities. The material presented in this book may offer additional help to families in locating the point at which their family is situated on the continuum of family competence. In doing so, family members may more clearly recognize the patterns that are associated with a certain level of competence.

If you have been able to locate the point on the continuum at which your family may be placed, the next question is, "What can you do about it?" The first step is to decide whether or not you wish to do anything about it. You may feel that no changes are necessary, that your family is healthy. Or you may feel that however troubled your family is, what goes on in the family is definite, certain, and predictable. An attempt to change may seem uncertain and even dangerous. There can be a good deal of pain involved in the attempt to change and, even under the best of circumstances, there may be a temporary period when things seem worse. So, the decision about whether or not to try to change when goes on in your family is a big one; only you can make it.

There are, however, compelling reasons to consider trying to change what goes on in your family. The first is that it is very difficult to be any happier than your family is. A person may be happier without a family than in a family, but if you are in a family it is difficult to be happy if what goes on in the family is often miserable. You can find good friends, an exciting job, or volunteer work, and these can be very important parts of your life, but if in the family you feel unloved, are constantly fighting, feel unimportant, or always seem to end up with all the responsibility, there is a very good possibility that you won't be happy much of the time.

Beyond happiness, however, is the matter of your mental health. There are several major factors that influence mental health. Heredity is one. Childhood experiences are another. Large social stresses like poverty and discrimination are another. The family with all that goes on in it, however, is an especially important factor that influences your mental health. Its importance is related to the fact that what goes on in the family is easier to change than the influence of heredity, childhood experiences, or social deprivation. The latter factors can be understood and, under some circumstances, modified, but in general they are not as easy to change as the relationships within your family. To put it another way, the relationship within your family may be hard to change, but the other factors are often much more difficult for the individual to get a handle on and change directly.

The scientific evidence indicating that a person's family influences his or her mental health, continues to mount. Although people in healthy families can develop serious depressions or other major psychiatric disturbances because of heredity, childhood experiences, or social stress, family discord is the most common final link in the chain of events leading to mental illness.

Indeed, one of the two central jobs of the family is to protect the mental health of its family members. The research findings upon which the continuum of family competence was constructed indicated that the members of healthy families were well adjusted individuals, and that troubled and severely troubled families often contained one or more individuals with psychiatric disturbances. Moreover, seriously troubled families, on average, are much more apt to contain one or more seriously disturbed family members than are troubled families. In other words, often there is a relationship between the degree of family disturbance and the seriousness of family members' psychiatric disturbances.

The decision as to whether or not to make a serious attempt to change what goes on in your family is an important decision. The weight of the evidence suggests that both personal happiness and individual mental health can be influenced by the decision. On the other hand, there are risks in trying to change one's family, and each person must balance those risks against what may be gained through the effort to change.

If you have decided that the effort to change your family is either desirable or necessary, how do you go about it? Although family change may require a great deal of every family member, some general principles can be suggested.

1) *Focus initially on the parents' relationship.* One of the principal factors that separates healthy families from all others is the nature of the parents' relationship. Two aspects of the relationship are particularly important: power and intimacy. The couples in healthy families share power and achieve, at times, the intimate level of communication. The parents in all other families do not either share power or achieve intimate communication. Many fail to do both, for the sharing of power is powerfully conducive to the establishment of intimate communication.

Often a husband or wife will seek help and state emphatically that his or her spouse denies the existence of a problem and shows no inclination to change or seek help. This can be a difficult problem because frequently the resistant spouse is afraid that the relationship is hopeless or that he or she is incapable of accomplishing the necessary changes. Most commonly, however, the couple has been caught up in blaming each other for the difficulties in the relationship. The pattern of blame and attack can be firmly entrenched, and stopping it is the important first step. This can happen only if both husband and wife accept the fact that each has participated in the development of the distressed relationship and each must shoulder a part of the responsibility. "We're both responsible for our relationship" is the type of statement that suggests a couple is ready to work on improving their relationship. Often, the spouse who complains that his or her mate will not agree to try to change the relationship is not reporting accurately, but rather continuing to blame the spouse for the deficiencies in the relationship.

If you and your mate are beyond the stage of blame and attack, the next consideration involves the joint attempt to appraise how you deal with power and intimacy. "Who has the right to decide what?" is an important question. "How do we deal with our differences?" is another. If one person has a disproportionate share of the power, it is generally because both individuals initially wanted or needed it that way. If differences are never really settled or if the couple has never learned to negotiate with each other, the suggestion is strong that there is either unequal distribution of power or conflict about power. Negotiation is suggested if the couple often reaches a compromise when confronted with strong differences.

Intimacy—the ability to let each other know truly deep feelings and thoughts—is suggested if there are no secrets. Secrets are an impediment to intimate communication and, most often, represent, "If you knew how I really felt, you'd put me down, reject, or make fun of me." Although each person does have the right to privacy, it is the ability of the couple to communicate at this level, at least some of the time, that is important.

In effect, it can be helpful for the couple to look at their relationship together and assess its strengths and weaknesses. This is a collaborative approach to the evaluation of one's family and uses as a starting point an assessment of the parents' relationship. Additional help in the evaluation of one's family can come about by locating the point on the family continuum at which one's family is located. There are some general principles about changing one's family that grow out of an awareness of how troubled one's family is.

2) *Become aware of the level of family competence.* If your family is severely troubled or chaotic, there is little likelihood that you can change your family without outside help. In the first place, severely troubled families have a strong tendency to deny that there is anything wrong. Even when life is chaotic, one or more family members significantly disturbed, and the outside world seen as terribly dangerous, the family clings together and holds tenaciously to the belief that there is nothing wrong. It is possible, therefore, that you will not recognize the description of severely troubled families as anything like your family. It is also likely that the murky "we-ness" that seriously hinders the development of individuality will push other members of the family to agree that there is absolutely nothing wrong with your family.

The help needed by a chaotic family must be very skilled. Not every professional who works with families has all that it takes to assist chaotic families to change and grow toward clearer family structure and greater individual autonomy. Chaotic families distrust outsiders and resist change, and it takes an extremely able family therapist to help the family work through its distrust, chaos, and fear of change. Even with such a therapist, change and growth usually take a great deal of time and effort. It is as if your family has a steep mountain to climb. You need an unusual guide and great courage to try. At the top of the mountain, however, there is a new kind of closeness that allows family members to be different, feelings to be expressed, problems to be recognized early and solved effectively, losses mourned, and joy discovered.

For the troubled families, there are different messages. If your pattern is one of dominance and submission, many of the messages must be directed to the dominant parent. First, are you lonely? Do you want sometimes to be out from under the awesome responsibility of running the whole show? Wouldn't it be great to feel that your wife or husband and older children are competent? Can you imagine not having to be on control, not having to take charge of everything you touch, and even sometimes letting others take care of you?

There are also questions for the submissive partner. Some of them are: Wouldn't you like to feel competent, to have greater self-confidence? Aren't you tired of always deferring to your husband's (wife's) judgment? Can you see the subtle ways in which you defeat him (or her): missing appointments, being late, forgetting checks you wrote, not having the automobile oil checked, secretly relishing your child's flaunting of your husband's (wife's) important rules . . .? The list of disguised, rebellious behaviors used by submissive partners is endless.

If dominance and submission are your family pattern, you need to consider how to change it. If life in the family really isn't what you want it to be, it can be changed. It is likely that you need outside help, but there is some possibility that you can do it yourselves. If both you and your mate desire a change, you may be able to change without an outside expert. The essential issue is the need to learn to negotiate. But don't hesitate to find the assistance of an expert. Change will not be easy, but remember the payoff. For your family, change can result in greater intimacy, shared responsibility, and less anger and sadness.

For those troubled families who have evolved a conflicted pattern, you need outside help—someone to teach you how to share power, negotiate differences, and establish mutually agreeable rules for your relationship. In this type of family, perhaps only the parents need marital therapy. If the husband and wife both are tired of the war, the chances are good that with help the relationship can be much better. The major task for both husband and wife is to learn to look at the conflict as a shared failure in the relationship. In this type of marital relationship, each spouse characteristically sees only the part the other plays. Each is blind to his or her own role and, as a consequence, there is no possibility of understanding the conflict as a shared responsibility. An outside expert is usually needed to break this impasse and assist initially in working out new ground rules for the relationship.

For faltering families, the central problem is the parents' failure to evolve a relationship in which intimate communication can occur. The wives in such families may obtain individual treatment for their unhappiness, anger, and depression. Although the individual treatment of wives from faltering families can be helpful, it is not aimed directly at the shared failure of wife and husband in establishing a gratifying relationship and, for that reason, may fail. Under many circumstances, it would be more appropriate for both husband and wife to be involved together in marital treatment. Although husbands from these families are often initially resistant, many will participate if the focus of the treatment is on the shared failure rather than solely on their role.

In a way, faltering families are tragic "near misses." They have many strengths—but still fall short of what healthy families demonstrate can be achieved.

The healthy families studied all seem to recognize their good fortune. Often, such families are truly perplexed about how they came to be so fortunate. Both husband and wife frequently give the major credit to each other. Research, however, does not suggest that they are correct in giving each other the major credit. Rather, together they have evolved a family in which individuality is encouraged, intimacy nourished, and personal meaning discovered. Such families tell us much about what is possible in human relationships.

3) *Accept the fact that family change takes time and courage.* Families gradually evolve certain patterns of relationships. Starting with the parents' marriage, a set of rules is elaborated. These, though rarely talked about, come to set the tempo and the basic mood of the family. The rules are in response to questions that each couple must answer. Some of the important questions are:

1. How are we going to make decisions?
2. How are we going to settle our differences?
3. How are we going to be true individuals and still achieve closeness?
4. How can we learn to share with each other our deepest feelings and thoughts?

5. How are we going to establish a sexual relationship that is satisfying to both of us?
6. How are we going to continue to feel close to each of our families and yet lead a life of our own?

These questions must be answered by each couple. They deal with the basic issues of power, intimacy, and self-determination. There are, of course, many other questions, the answers to which become part of the pattern of the relationship and, ultimately, determine the quality of life within the family. These patterns become entrenched; yet, if a family is to change and grow, it is precisely these patterns that must be altered. The attempt to change one's family, therefore, is an act of courage. It really takes a great deal of fortitude to try to change basic patterns within the family. It also takes time. Often, the earlier in a family's life that change is attempted, the less will be the resistance to change. It does require, however, an acceptance of the fact that change requires both time and courage.

In summary, this book may be used as a way of looking at your family. The book is based on both research findings with healthy families and clinical work with distressed families. Its value grows out of the fact that the lessons learned have come from families much like your own and those who live around you. The families studied were made up of people who wanted the best that life can offer for themselves and their families. For many, however, family life was dominated by relationship patterns established long ago—patterns that prevented the family members from achieving high levels of individuality and closeness, as well as a sense of personal value and meaning.

If there are obstacles to a healthy family life, they are these relationship patterns, not individual family members or the outside world. If we recognize the relationship patterns that get in the way of what we want and need, a critical first step has been taken. Rather than blaming each other, fate, or the world, we have, at that moment, started to use our intelligence to understand and change the most important world of all—the family world.

Recognizing one's family patterns is, by itself, not enough. A decision to change must be made and the responsibility is shared by the parents. Together they must decide whether or not to risk change. If the decision is to try to change, they must decide what changes are most needed. Not infrequently, going just this far in itself results in family change. Communication has been opened, responsibility shared, hope reborn. Such a process can gather momentum and lead to significant change.

Often, however, more work is necessary. Simple things need to be established—such as the parents taking time each day to talk privately about their relationship and life in their family. Both husband and wife must learn to listen to each other's comments, suggestions, and criticisms—with the assumption that they contain much that is important rather than disparaging them as worthless attacks. The children can be brought into some of the discussions, particularly as they reach adolescence. Although most often the couple has a great deal of work to do on their relationship—and this may best be done alone—the children can often be helpful. For the most part, they know what's going on and even if they are not a part of the solution, they may be reassured to know that their parents are working on their problems.

If you have come this far and, despite your efforts to improve things, your family remains troubled, get outside help. Go to your family doctor or clergyman, or call the local medical society, professional association, hospital, or university and get the names of qualified family therapists. Arrange for an initial interview and size up the professional. Does he or she seem to be a person that the family could trust to help the family change?

Commit yourselves to the idea that change is going to take time and will involve pain. Find within the courage to press on. One of the advantages of knowing something of what goes on in healthy families is that it tells us something of what is possible in family life. That can provide hope. Hope, of course, by itself is insufficient, but without it nothing is really possible.

This book is an attempt to translate psychiatric research into a form that is useful to families. To the extent that it helps clarify the relationship patterns that prevent families from achieving that which is possible and offers encouragement and hope to those who wish to try, it will have succeeded.

Index